Reading Games

Make Reading Fun

Reading Games Make Reading Fun

Reading Games for K-Grade 6

A Guide for Enriching Reading Skills
by
Joseph G. Bielawski

and
Lawrence Pomerleau

R D Communications
Georgetown, Connecticut

ISBN 0-914138-00-6

Illustrations: Guy M. Parker, Jr.
Typography: Graphic Arts Associates
Printing and Binding: Eastern Press, Inc.

Additional copies of this book may be ordered from:

RD Communications
PO Box 42
Georgetown, CT 06829

About the Authors

Joseph G. Bielawski brings to this guide his extesive experience as a teacher, author, editor, and creator of educational materals. He is presently Editor of Scholastic Magazines *News Pilot, News Ranger,* and *Merry-Go-Round* magazines for primary level students. He has created teaching materials for Scholastic, Western Publishing Company, Reader's Digest, and American Education Publications. As a teacher, his experience ranges from elementary classroom teaching and service as a Reading Consultant to college level instruction. His previous books include *My Country, U.S.A., We Need Each Other, Guide to Educational Technology: Early Childhood Education.*

Lawrence W. Pomerleau is Reading Consultant for the Greenwich (Connecticut) Public Schools and is a veteran of over twenty years of teaching. He is a member of the Advisory Board of Scholastic Elementary Magazines and is active in the International Reading Association, the Executive Board of the Connecticut Reading Conference, the Connecticut Education Association, and the Boy Scouts of America.

INTRODUCTION

How do we learn? In a combination or variety of ways, determined initially by our self-concept, which affects practically all that we do. A good self-concept gives us confidence in ourselves to learn, to cooperate, to be a responsible individual.

There are many ways in which we can help a child to gain confidence in himself. In learning to read, games help many children build confidence. There is no need in game participation to fear failure, rejection, or criticism. A child can achieve status by having some skill that can become his or her specialty.

Active participation in games can help a child to gain self-control, and to practice discipline that is reasonable, fair, consistent. In many games, affection and friendship are expressed. Taking care of components of a game (and its proper storage) helps a child to develop responsible behavior—being careful in using and storing without unnecessary damage. By creating and using games, a child feels responsible for attending to his (and his classmates) personal belongings. In many games, a child develops leadership in playing, or teaching others how to play. In addition, games tend to help children to be orderly when not under close supervision.

In learning how to read, a child develops an entire hierarchy of abilities, and these skills are developed gradually. Essential to reading success (and other language arts) is skill in auditory and visual perception. Without these skills, learning to use other word recognition skills is impossible. Many children who are reluctant or disinterested in skill building are easily motivated by games.

Using games (and other approaches) for enriching word recognition skills begins in preschool and sometimes continues into high school, since there is no limit to the skill in word recognition that can be acquired. Skill in word recognition takes time, sequence, continuity, and integration of word recognition skills to insure competence. Higher-level word recognition skills are not stepped-up lower-level skills done faster. They are attained by a step-by-step ascending scale of difficulty and application. Without competence in these skills, a child cannot read fluently, read with understanding, interpret what is read, nor enjoy reading. Word recognition skills can make the difference between failure and success in school.

A child who is happily involved in activities that are satisfying and meaningful is too busy to waste time or become a discipline problem. Learning through game-playing is an excellent way to keep a child involved.

The 250 games in this book provide a rewarding program of activities to supplement and enrich your reading program—regardless of the approach you use. The games provide assistance in individualizing instruction and in extending reading activities.

Arrangement and Use

The Guide contains a treasure of suggestions for reading activities on different grade levels, with a great variety of approaches to games. They are arranged in a sequence of difficulty, and whenever possible, examples and illustrations have been included.

Games are listed by specific major skill and subskill (see Table of Contents). They:
- can be used for diagnosis, reinforcement, or post testing
- provide variety and fun, fundamental to a good reading program
- provide for individual activities geared to help a particular child or group
- can be adapted to the needs of an individual or group by substitution of vocabulary or certain rules of a game
- can be played without equipment or equipment that can be made inexpensively and kept in accessible classroom storage

Under each major skill and subskill, each game is listed by:
1. Title of Game
2. Level: (P) Primary or (I) Intermediate
3. Number of Players
4. Materials (if any are needed)
5. Directions for Game Playing
6. Variations or Crossreference (if any)

In games where equipment is needed, encourage and help children to make the components, or enlist the assistance of pupils in an upper grade. Provide a particular place where games are to be stored upon completion of their use, and assign responsibility to pupils for keeping the games in good condition. In many instances, pupils will want to make their own version of a game which would be similar to one they have played or mastered.

Introduce the games so children will know how to play a game, its objectives, and how it may help them in reading—by playing a game alone, in pairs, or in small groups, without teacher supervision.

As each game is introduced, you may want to put it on a 5" x 7" card and set up a classroom file where children can select individual cards for individual or group participation, without teacher attention.

CONTENTS

I. PERCEPTION AND WORD ANALYSIS

A. INITIAL CONSONANT SOUNDS

1. Make a Match (P)   (Individual or Pair)

Materials: 2 sets of cards—one set of 21 consonant-letter cards; second set of 21 picture cards, each picture-word beginning with a different consonant sound.

Directions: (Individual) Match each letter card with the corresponding picture card. (Pair) Each player has a set of cards. They take turns matching a letter card with a picture card. The player who identifies the most pairs wins the game.

Variations: Similar game cards can be made for blends, digraphs, and entire alphabet. Let Players help to construct the materials for the games, or have players in upper grades assist.

2. What Will You Take? (P) (I)   (Small or large group)

Materials: none

Directions: One player begins by saying, "I am going to Maine." The second player repeats the sentence and adds a second sentence, as, "I am going to Maine. I will take a monkey." In turn, each player repeats the initial sentence and must add a second sentence which includes taking something that begins with **m**. The game is continued among those players who gave an incorrect answer and have not discovered the **m** clue.

Variation: Use name places to provide practice with other beginning consonant sounds, as Baltimore, Denver, Florida, etc.

3. Shop at the Supermarket (P) (Small or large group)

Materials: none

Directions: The first player says, "I have been to the super-market. I bought a package of bacon. Who has bought something else that begins with the same sound as bacon?" Continue with a new game-leader and another word, such as milk.

4. I Am Thinking (P) (I) (2 or more players or teams)

Materials: Make word cards and put them in a chart holder or post them on a bulletin board.

Directions: The first player begins by saying, "I am thinking of a word." The next player asks, "Is it . . . ?" and suggests one of the cards in the chart. The game continues until one of the players names the correct card. The child who guessed correctly begins the next game and continues in the same way.

5. Let Your Ears Tell You (P) (2 or more players or teams)

Materials: Sentence strips, such as (1) Paul picked up a pile of papers. (2) Donna had a dollar and a dime. (3) Gary got good grades. (4) Larry likes lettuce.

Directions: The sentence strips are evenly divided between the players or teams. The first player or team reads the sentence on one strip and asks the opposing player or team to identify the re-peated sound or letter in the sentence. The player or team with the larger number of correct answers wins. The game can be ex-tended by having players write a variation of sentence strips that are alliterative.

6. Spin for Consonants (P)   (Individual; 2 or more teams)

Materials: Consonant wheel from Spin-a-Word Game No. 53.

Directions: Players take turns as they spin for a consonant and then give a word that begins with the same consonant. Each player receives 1 point for each correct answer. No points are given to a player who doesn't give a correct reply. The player or team with the most points wins the game.

7. Beginning Sounds (P)   (Individual; 2 persons or teams)

Materials: Make a set of alphabet cards. On a second set of cards, write words that the players have had in their reading or sight vocabulary (pictures can be added if desirable).

Directions: A player or team matches a word card with the letter card that has the beginning letter of the word. The player or team with the most pairs of cards wins the game.

8. Up the Ladder (P) (I)   (Individual; 2 or more players or teams)

Materials: Draw two ladders on the chalkboard or on individual sheets of paper. The first ladder contains words that you assign.

Directions: Players must fill in the second ladder to "climb" to the top by giving a word that begins with the initial consonant of each key word on the respective rungs of the first ladder. A timed race can be planned when two or more players or teams use the game. [*See following illustration.*]

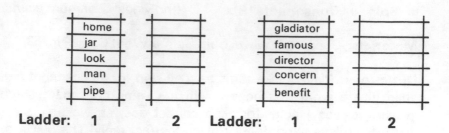

Ladder: 1   2   **Ladder:** 1   2

9. Words That Begin the Same (P)   (2 or more players)

Materials: Sheet of paper and pencil for each player.

Directions: Each player writes a list of words (5 or 10, depending on abilities) that begin with various consonants at the left side of the paper. Each paper is exchanged. Players must then write another word (that begins with the same consonant) beside each word in the list.

10. Letter Dominoes (P) (I)   (2 or more players or teams)

Materials: Use a dozen or two of 3 x 5" cards, and write two consonant letters on each card (see below).

Directions: The first player sets down a domino-card. The second player must match a letter on the card with the same letter on another card.

Variations: Other sets of domino-cards can be made just with pictures, single words, or phrases.

11. Name Game (P)   (2 or more players or teams)

Materials: Name card for each player.

Directions: On a table or chalk tray, each player puts his or her name in the correct group according to sex.

Variations: Name cards of players may be placed in piles according to hair or eye color; related to various class activities that are related.

12. Sentence Races (P) (I)   (2 or more players-partners)

Materials: Paper and pencils for each pair of partners.

Directions: Partners try to write a "real" sentence in which each word begins with the same consonant. Examples: Tom Taylor took two toys to Topeka. Six silly sailors sang seven sea songs. At the end of a given period, the sentences are read. The partners who have the longest (or most) "real" sentences in which all words begin with **t** or **s** win a point.

Variation: The game can be played where every word need not begin with the same consonant. In this game, a point can be given for each word in the sentence that does begin with the same consonant.

13. Telegrams (I)   (2 or more players or teams)

Materials: Sheet of paper and pencil for each player or team.

Directions: A leader is chosen and dictates 5-10 letters at random. Each player or team must compose a telegram, using these same letters as the beginning letter of each word.
Example: S — T — B — C — M — P — I — H

T E L E G R A M
Send twenty big crackers. My parrot is hungry.

14. Beanbag Toss (P)   (2 or more players)

Materials: A beanbag; sheet of butcher paper marked into equal squares with a different consonant written in each square.

Directions: Place the paper on the floor. In turn, each player tosses the bag, and pronounces the letter the bag has landed on. The player then suggests a word that begins with that same letter. Allow 2 points for each correct letter and word given.

Variations: This same game can be used for digraphs, blends, words, etc. in place of single consonants. Classification headings can also be substituted for single consonants in the squares.

15. Heads and Tails (P)   (2 or more players)

Materials: Make a set of cards, each containing a vocabulary word (on the both sides) that needs practice. See illustration.

Directions: The cards are divided among players. The first player flips a card. If it "lands" heads, the next player must suggest a word that begins with the same consonant. If the card "lands" tails, the next player must suggest a word that ends with the same consonant. After a correct answer is given, the next player takes a turn at flipping a card. If an incorrect answer is given, the player loses a turn.

| Heads
 YELLOW | y | ROBIN

     Tails | n |

16. Initial Consonant Bingo (P)   (Small or large group)

Materials: Make a set of Bingo-type cards, each with various consonants; bits of paper or cardboard for markers.

Directions: The game is played just like "Bingo." As the caller mentions a word, the players cover the correct initial consonant if it is on their cards.

Variations: In place of consonants, substitute digraphs, blends, words, or pictures.

B. FINAL CONSONANT SOUNDS

17. Relay Teams (P) (I)   (2 or more teams of 3-6 players)

Materials: Chalksticks and Chalkboard.

Directions: Players form teams. The first player of each team writes a word on the chalkboard. In turn, each team member adds a word below the preceding one. The added word must begin with the last letter of the previous word. The team that completes a "real" sentence in which each player has written a word wins the game. Example: Five eagles saw wild dogs.

18. Make It Grow (I)   (Individual or group)

Materials: Sheet of paper and pencil for each child.

Directions: In this final-consonant game, each succeeding word begins with the same consonant as the one with which the previous one ended. A player answers the statements to form the patterns. When 2 or more players are involved, you can make a speed race of this game. Example: (1) Four-legged animal that barks (2) Flowers are grown here (3) Birds build them in trees (4) A food seasoning.

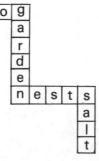

Variation: For less-able players, use picture clues for answering or doing the pattern (dog, goose, eggs).

19. How Does It End? (P)   (1 or more players)

Materials: Set of boxed picture cards and 3 letters for each.

Directions: A player pronounces the name of each picture and decides which letter stands for the ending sound.

k   l   b

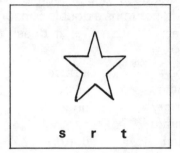

s   r   t

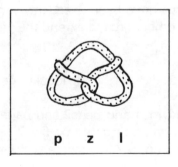

p   z   l

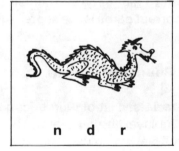

n   d   r

C. SPECIAL CONSONANT SOUNDS

20. Double or Nothing   (1 or more pairs of players)

Materials: List of words (see below); pencil and paper for score keeping.

Directions: One player has a list of words which he or she pronounces (one at a time). The second player tells whether the word contains a double consonant or not — saying, "Double" if it does; "Nothing" if it doesn't. Score 1 point for each correct answer.

rabbit	lettuce	running	cabbage
ladder	pillow	racing	arrow
hungry	finger	tapping	mummy
funny	happy	buzzing	family
listen	cotton	reading	lesson

Variation: Instead of a list of words, individual cards — each with a printed word can be used. When a player is correct, the card is given to him or her. When all cards have been used, the number of correct cards is the score. Add other cards to extend the game.

21. Sounds of C (P) (I)   (Individual or group)

Materials: List of words (can be Ditto) and pencil and paper for each player. If you prefer, the list can be printed on 5 x 7" card, and a player can use a blank sheet of paper to indicate answers.

Directions: A player receives a list (or card) of words containing c. In some words, **c** has the hard sound as in **cow**. In other words, **c** has the soft sound as in **celery**. The player is to classify the words according to sound under the correct headings:

C AS IN COW .... C AS IN CELERY

cake	candy	cap	city	cent
cage	camel	calf	center	cider
come	cave	cone	cellar	cement
bacon	comic	plastic	mice	place
cork	actor	cube	race	recent

Variation: For a more elementary game, make 2 picture cards for each player (see below). As you call out words containing **c,** players hold up the correct picture card to indicate which sound of **c** they hear.

 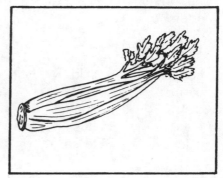

22. G as in Giant (P) (I) (Individual or group)

Materials: Same as in Game 21, except for word list (see below).

Directions: Same as in Game 21, except that in some words, **g** has the hard sound as in **gate**. In other words, **g** has the soft sound as in **giraffe**.

G AS IN GATE ....G AS IN GIRAFFE

game	garden	gem	gentle
gave	gather	germs	age
gold	geese	gypsy	ginger
gift	wig	bridge	engine
rug	bag	magic	cage

23. Sounds of S (P) (I)   (Individual or group)

Materials: Same as in Game 21, except for word list (see below).

Directions: Same as in Game 21, except that in some words, **s** has the sound as in **sit**. In other words, **s** has the sound as in **nose**.

S AS IN SIT ....S AS IN NOSE

sad	said	dogs	birds
same	seal	rise	six
sick	some	cause	please
glass	bus	trees	raisin
ducks	lesson	wise	rose

Variation: Some rules as in Game 21. For (I) groups, you might use other sounds of **s** as in the following words:

sugar	pleasure	season	leisure
treasure	surprise	reason	scissors
measure	session	lesson	possession

To reinforce skills in Games 21, 22, and 23, you might make a wheel and spinner as for Game 53 (vowel wheel). Divide the circle into 6 equal parts, using a picture and a letter in each: c—cow; g—giraffe; s—sun; c—celery; g—gate; s—2 birds. Players spin the arrow and suggest another word that has the same **s, g,** or **c** - sound as the picture word indicated on the wheel.

24. Hands Up! (P) (Small or large group)

Materials: List of words (see below).

Directions: One player is the leader. He or she reads the list of words one at a time, and says, "Hands Up." The other players raise their hands if they know the middle consonant in the word. Extend the game by adding other words to the list, or make separate lists on 5 x 7" cards.

summer (M)	rabbit (B)	cannot (N)	turkey (R or K)
little (T)	dollar (L)	camel (M)	garden (R or D)
hurry (R)	minnow (N)	yellow (L)	fourteen (R or T)
supper (P)	lovely (V)	moment (M)	husband (S or B)
water (T)	valley (L)	rubber (B)	window (N or D)

25. Sounds of qu, x and ph (P) (I) (1 or more players)

Materials: On a 5 x 7" card, list the headings of **f, ks,** and **kw.** Then add a list of words that contain an **x, ph,** or **qu.**

Directions: On a separate sheet of paper, players copy the three headings and then list the words under the heading that contains the same sound. (In most words, **qu** has the sound of **kw** as in queen; **x** has the sound of **ks** as in tax; **ph** has the sound of **f** as in phone.

fox	photo	Ralph	box
Philip	taxi	axe	elephant
extra	phlox	quick	pheasant
next	wax	quart	quiet
fix	quack	six	phonograph

26. Y as a Consonant (P)   (Individual or group)

Materials: List of words containing **y** (see below); pencil and paper for each player.

Directions: A player crosses out the **y** in each word where the **y** has the sound of the preceding vowel (or is silent).

you	tray	player	yet
stay	yes	clay	young
today	yesterday	youth	yellow

27. Sounds of ed (P) (I)   (1 or more players)

Materials: Make a list of words and three headings (t, d, ed); pencil and paper for each player.

Directions: A player lists the following words under the correct heading. (In some words, **ed** has the sound as in **rested**; the sound of **t** as in **raced**; the sound of **d** as in **loaned**.

hunted	farmed	carted	talked
landed	leaned	wanted	tried
darted	cried	dented	danced
started	dreamed	waited	scratched

D. CONSONANT DIGRAPHS

28. Spin the Arrow (P)   (2 or more players or teams)

Materials: Make a cardboard circle and arrow. Print consonant digraphs around the circle edge (see below).

Directions: Players take turns spinning the arrow. A player suggests a word that has the same beginning digraph.

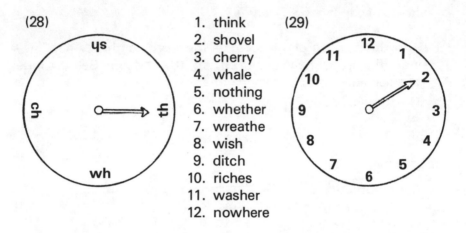

(28)

1. think
2. shovel
3. cherry
4. whale
5. nothing
6. whether
7. wreathe
8. wish
9. ditch
10. riches
11. washer
12. nowhere

(29)

29. Wheel of Chance (P) (I)   (Individual; 2 or more players)

Materials: Use a large clock face made from cardboard. On the chalkboard (or 5 x 7″ card) print 12 words containing a consonant digraph (see above).

Directions: Each player spins the clock hand (in turn) and checks the number on which it stops. The player then reads a word with the corresponding digraph from the board or card. Extend the game by having players use the word in a sentence (for an extra score point).

Variation: Use the clock face and words that contain consonant blends.

30. Two Letters, One Sound (P) (I)   (Individual; 2 or more players)

Materials: Lists of words containing consonant digraphs — on sheets of paper or 5 x 7″ cards.

Directions: Each player rewrites the words on his or her list — under the proper headings of **ch, sh, th,** and **wh.** See the Index for selected words containing digraphs.

E. CONSONANT BLENDS

31. Name the Blend (P)   (2 or more players or teams)

Materials: Use the same materials as for Game 28, but substitute consonant blends for the digraphs.

Directions: Same as for Game 28.

32. Match the Blend (P)   (Individual; 2 or more players)

Materials: Make a set of 38 picture cards (or 19 pairs), each pair of pictures should have names which begin with a different blend. See the Index for a list of picture words.

Directions: For individual play, all cards are turned face up, and the player arranges the cards in pairs (according to initial blend). For group play, cards are dealt among players, and played in the same way as the "Old Maid" card game. The player or team with the most pairs wins the game.

33. Think Fast and Write (P) (I)   (2 or more players or teams)

Materials: Paper and pencil for each player; list of headings for the leader (See the Index for list of words).

Directions: One player is the leader who calls out a heading. The rest of the players or teams list as many words as they can in a given period of time (a minute or two). The player or team with the most correct answers wins the game Suggested headings: bl, br, cl, cr, dr, fl, fr, gl, gr, pl, pr, sk, sl, sm, sn, sp, st, sw, tr. See the Index for list of blends.

Variation: The same type of game can be used with digraphs, initial letters, and classification.

34. Find the Blend (P) (I)   (1 or more players)

Materials: Ditto sheets of pictures and blends for each player.

Directions: A player names the picture word and then writes the blend to show whether it appears at the beginning, middle, or end of the word.

F. SILENT LETTERS

35. Find Each Silent Consonant (P) (I)   (1 or more players or teams)

Materials: Make a Ditto list of words, each of which contains one or more silent consonants.

Directions: A player silently pronounces each word and draws a line through each silent consonant. Examples:

comb	rabbit	calf	high
school	lamb	dumb	wrong
night	light	sight	subtle
half	kitten	thumb	knight

Variation: When a player is familiar with vowels and vowel sounds, provide a list of words, each of which contains one or more silent letters (both consonant and vowel). Examples: aim, life, rain, seed, read, write, knife.

36. Now You Hear It — Now You Don't

Materials: Make a list of words in which each word contains a consonant such as b, k, w, gh.

Directions: A player silently reads each word and draws a line through the silent consonants. For group play, a leader pronounces each word and the other players write the silent consonant in each word.

comb	thought	bacon	thorough
barn	ghost	numb	combine
cattle	king	written	tomorrow
write	huge	reward	unknown
waste	throw	knife	knowledge
know	window	kindle	wrinkle

G. VOWELS

37. What Do You Hear? (P) (I)   (2 or more players)

Materials: List of words containing short vowel sounds for the leader; paper and pencil for each player.

Directions: The leader pronounces each word on the list. Players number their paper and write the vowel they hear in each word.

best	frog	rapid	basket
cat	brick	trust	better
pig	dress	print	pocket
tub	plum	felt	pickle
dog	track	drugs	tablet

38. Long Vowel Sounds (P) (I)   (Individual or group)

Materials: Ditto list of words and pencil for each player.

Directions: A player writes the vowel he or she hears (after each word):

goat	sail	use
mean	meat	toe
pail	soap	they
tale	tree	boat
stay	cube	peach
bone	soul	train

39. Short and Long Vowels (P)   (1 or more players)

Materials: Make Ditto sheets of picture words with letters as indicated below; pencil for each child.

Directions: A player circles the correct vowel that is in the picture-word name.

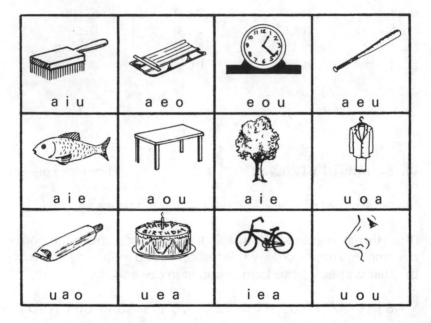

a i u	a e o	e o u	a e u
a i e	a o u	a i e	u o a
u a o	u e a	i e a	u o u

Variation: Use the same type of game, but include only pictures whose names contain a short vowel sound; a long vowel sound.

40. Vowel Spin (P)   (1 or more players or teams)

Materials: Vowel letter wheel (see Game No. 53).

Directions: Players take turns as they spin a vowel and give a word that contains the same short or long vowel sound. Same scoring as in "Spin for Consonants," Game No. 6.

41. Making Words (P)   (1 or more players)

Materials: Ditto sheet of words and pencil for each player.

Directions: Each player writes a vowel in the space to make a word:

c__t	r__n	h__d	w__ng
b__t	h__n	b__d	s__ng
s__t	p__n	d__d	b__ng
g__t	s__n	c__d	th__ng
p__t	c__n	m__d	sw__ng

42. Sounds of Y (Vowel)   (1 or more players)

Materials: List of words and pencil for each player.

Directions: A player lists the following words under the correct heading. In some words, **y** has a short sound as in **lady** and **kitty**. In other words, **y** has a long sound as in **cry** and **fly**

Y AS IN LADY AND KITTY . . . . .Y AS IN CRY AND FLY

funny	buy	sly	tricky
dry	beauty	candy	try
deny	story	daisy	busy
rainy	reply	bunny	why
eye	style	fry	lazy
my	early	city	lying
supply	happy	hungry	sleepy

43. Mixed-up Vowel Sounds (P) (I)   (1 or more players)

Materials: Make a Ditto list of headings and words as shown below.

Directions: Players are to list each word under the correct heading.

Headings:	Short a as in hat	Long a as in lake	a as in star	a as in call
Words:	take	ball	name	barn
	that	can	saw	sad
	march	hard	farm	small

Variation: Make a separate list for other vowel sounds.

44. Vowel Ladder (P) (I)   (Individual or group)

Materials: Make two make-believe ladders on the chalkboard. (See Game No. 8.)

Directions: Starting from the bottom of the first ladder, the leader reads the words and the players respond with a word that begins and ends in the same way (lake — lace).

5. about
4. rain
3. jump
2. around
1. land

Variation: For more able players, use a higher level of vocabulary.

45. Vowel Houses (P)   (group)

Materials: Draw four houses in a row on the chalkboard. Choose a doorkeeper for the first three houses. Label the houses as indicated below (if the drill is on short vowels or longs vowels).

Directions: The leader whispers a word to the first player (example: match). The player must select the right house on which to knock. The player asks the doorkeeper, "May I sleep in your house tonight?" The doorkeeper answers, "Yes, if you have the right name." The player answers, "I'm match." If the player is correct, the doorkeeper writes the player's initials in the house, and the game continues with the next player. If a player goes to the wrong house, he must sleep in the junk house (and write his initials there). If a doorkeeper makes a mistake, he or she loses the post to the player.

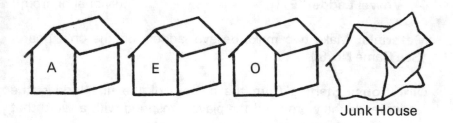

Junk House

46. Word Pyramids (I)

(1 or more players)

Materials: Card or sheet of paper with a single vowel written at the top; pencil for each player.

Directions: A player starts by reading the vowel and then adds one letter at a time—making a word with each letter added.

a	o
at	on
ate	one
team	once
steam	ounce
master	bounce

47. Picture Crossword (P)

(individual)

Materials: Ditto sheet of pictures, puzzles, and directions; pencil for each player.

Directions: The player is to name the pictures. Then he puts the correct name of each picture in the right boxes.

48. Vowel Crossword (I)

Materials: Ditto sheet of puzzle and clues; directions; pencil.

Directions: The player reads each clue. Then he puts the correct answers in the right boxes of the puzzle.

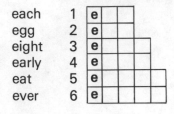

each	1
egg	2
eight	3
early	4
eat	5
ever	6

1. The chicken laid an___.
2. Did you___your lunch?
3. ___girl had a doll.
4. Did you___ride a train?
5. I woke up at___o'clock.
6. Let's try to get there___.

Variation: Let players construct other vowel puzzles for **a**, **i**, **o**, and **u**.

49. Vowel Combinations (P) (I)

(2 or more players)

Materials: Chalk and chalkboard; headings written on board.

Directions: Players take turns writing (under correct heading) another word that has the same vowel sound.
Headings: TRAIN, WEEK, BOAT, LAW, BOY, HOUSE, CAR, FOR, HER

50. Vowels and Sounds (individual)

Materials: Ditto sheet of headings and words for the player; pencil.

Directions: The player pronounces the heading (word) and then circles each word below that has the same vowel sound.

TRAIN

take	mate
chain	save
track	maid
sail	rain
lake	date

WEEK

meat	test
leaf	seal
bed	wet
feed	beans
peach	peek

BOAT

road	hole
hope	rode
coat	goat
top	cook
rock	vote

LAW

saw	lake
plane	hawk
paw	rain
claw	salt
Paul	fault

BOY

joy	oil
toy	join
coin	point
road	sole
lion	Roy

HOUSE

cow	now
loud	mouse
drum	out
south	cloud
owl	down

CAR

cart	star
park	mark
march	tar
stare	pear
part	jar

FOR

horn	floor
most	sorry
corn	story
horse	door
more	storm

HER

burn	bird
germ	fur
first	worm
porch	shirt
church	term

H. SUBSTITUTIONS (VOWEL AND CONSONANT)

51. Up and Down (P) (I)   (1 or more players)

Materials: Ditto sheet and pencil for each player (see below).

Directions: Each player writes words beginning and ending with the letters at the left:

F_____R		F	ou	R
A_____E		A	t	E
T_____H		T	eac	H
H_____T		H	a	T
E_____A		E	mm	A
R_____F		R	oo	F

52. Tick-Tack-Toe (P)   (2 or more players)

Materials: Paper and pencil for players.

Directions: Each player sketches a "Tick-Tack-Toe" square on his paper. The first player calls out a letter of the alphabet. All players write the letter in any space of his "Tick-Tack-Toe" square. Then the other players call out other letters (in turn) until all spaces of the square are filled. The player forming the most words with the called letters wins. Words can be read across, down, and diagonally.

53. Spin-a-Word (P) (Individual; 2 or more players)

Materials: 2 letter wheels, 2 spinners, letter cards: see below.

Directions: Separate cards along perforations. Use paper fastener to hold a spinner on a wheel. Then place letter cards (face up). Players use both spinners as they choose to spell a word. They take matching letter cards and place them in sequence to spell out a word. Once a word has been formed, letter cards are returned for other players' use. Score 1 point for 3-letter words; 2 points for 4-letter words; 3 points for 5-or-more-letter words. The player or team with most points wins.

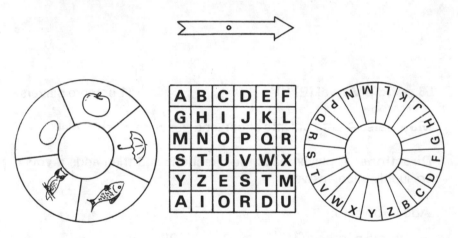

54. Rotating Wheel (P) (2 or more players or teams)

Materials: Make two circles (one smaller than the other). Fasten them together at the centers to rotate freely. Print consonant letters on the large circle, and phonograms around the edge of the smaller circle, so that different words can be lined up or formed.

Directions: In turn, each player rotates the larger circle and pronounces the word formed—and then uses it in a sentence for a score of 2 points.

55. Change the Vowel/Consonant (P) (I)   (2-5 players)

Materials: Make a list of key words on a 5 X 7" card for the leader.

Directions: The leader writes a key word on the chalkboard. Each player takes a turn in writing the same word except for the initial consonant, which must be supplied. Key Words: **B**all, **T**ell, **C**ake, **P**ot.

Variation: Use key words where players must supply another vowel: R**a**t, S**i**t, N**e**t, H**u**g, H**o**g.

56. Add a Vowel (P) (I)   (1 or more players)

Materials: A card or Ditto sheet, and pencil for each player.

Directions: A player reads the directions and then adds a vowel to supply each answer.

Add a vowel to:

1. make a purple fruit   PL___M
2. make the opposite of sit   ST___ND
3. make the opposite of boy   G___RL
4. make the same as large   B___G
5. make the same as little   SM___LL

Variations: Have individual pupils make additional cards of their own choosing.

· 57. Add a Letter (P) (I)   (1 or more players)

Materials: Same as for Game 56.

Directions: A player reads the directions and then adds a letter (or 2) to supply each answer.

Add a letter to:

1. make an insect   ___NT
2. make five plus four   N___NE
3. make an animal that crows   ___OOSTER
4. make the opposite of NO   YE_____
5. make the opposite of BRIDE   ___OOM

I. RHYME

58. What Doesn't Rhyme? (P)   (2 or more players)

Materials: List of rhyming words.

Directions: The leader pronounces a series of words that rhyme and one that doesn't rhyme. Players clap their hands when they hear the non-rhyming word.

Examples:

1. rat, fat, cat, go, bat
2. can, ran, man, fan, boy
3. bag, lip, gag, hag, nag
4. all, can, call, ball
5. ten, den, bend, hen
6. old, bold, cold, cat
7. sing, bring, Tim, ring
8. about, scout, bat, shout
9. dead, told, red, bed
10. gown, down, crown, spoon

59. What's My Name? (P)   (2 or more players)

Materials: none.

Directions: One player pronounces a word that rhymes with a name, and the other players try to guess the name.
Example: What's my name? It rhymes with hall. My name is (Paul).

Variations: Use last names; say the name twice and finish the rhyme: Ben, Ben lost his **pen**. Bill, Bill ran up the **hill**.

60. Jack-in-the-Box (P) (2 or more players)

Materials: List of words.

Directions: Players stand when the leader pronounces two words that rhyme. They remain seated when the pair of words do not rhyme. Any player who stands or sits at the wrong time is out of the game.
Examples: bad—say; sold—bad; pin—tin; girl—curl; bet—bat; sell—bell; fan—man; back—bold; flower—shower

Variation: See Game No. 58.

61. Bounce-a-Rhyme (P) (1 or more players)

Materials: Balls to bounce.

Directions: Each player begins with a ball and a starter word, such as land. Players bounce the ball and say a word that rhymes with the starter word for as long as they can. The player who bounces the ball and says the most words wins. (Starter words: can, cold, bit, day, will, set, bet, ten, bill, pack)

Variation: See Game No. 63

62. Treasure Chest (P) (2 or more players)

Materials: Treasure chest with objects that make noise, such as bells, plastic glasses, jars with objects in them, cymbals, rhythm instruments.

Directions: Players take two objects and make two separate noises in the chest. Other players tell if the noises are the same or different.

63. Rhyming Teams (P) (2 or more teams)

Materials: Paper, pencil, and starter words.

Directions: Players are grouped into teams. Each team is given a starter word, such as ball. Allow three minutes for each team to list words that rhyme with the starter word. The team having the largest number of rhyming words wins.

64. Is It . . . ? (P) (2 or more players)

Materials: List of words on cards or chalkboard.

Directions: The leader starts by saying, "I am thinking of a word that rhymes with (and gives a word that rhymes with a word on the board or cards). The next player says, "Is it . . . ?" and names one of the words on the board or cards. If the player guesses, then he becomes the leader.

Variation: Each player has word cards. The first player says a word, and each player holds up a word that rhymes with that word—if he has one.

65. Rhyme and Pantomime (P) (2 or more players or teams)

Materials: none.

Directions: The first team chooses a word and gives the other team a rhyming word of the chosen word as a clue. The second team pantomimes words that rhyme with the given word until they guess the chosen word of the first team.

66. Think of a Word (P)　　　　　　　　(2 or more players)

Materials: List of riddles about words.

Directions: Each player reads a riddle and the other players try to guess the word. Examples: Think of a word that rhymes with:

1. **sock**　You tell time with it. (clock)
2. **for**　You open it to enter a house. (door)
3. **now**　It gives milk. (cow)
4. **bat**　It is something you wear. (hat)
5. **spoon**　It shines in the sky. (moon)

67. Rhyme Bingo (P)　　　　　　　　(2 or more players)

Materials: Bingo cards with words, small cards with words that rhyme with the bingo-card words.

Directions: Players cover words that rhyme with the words called by the leader. The first player to cover five words horizontally, diagonally, or vertically wins.

Example:

R	H	Y	M	E
ball	few	ring	ear	bet
mess	can	far	bug	well
pie	run	FREE	up	law
and	in	ill	it	ten
wish	old	big	at	few

68. Rhyming Dominoes (P) (I)   (2 or more players)

Materials: Dominoes with words that rhyme.

Directions: Players match the words that rhyme on one domino with the words on another domino. See Game No. 10.

69. Make Them Rhyme (I)   (1 or more players)

Materials: Groups of four words that rhyme.

Directions: Players are given four rhyming words. They write lines using the four rhyming words. Examples: sky, fly, by, cry.

Up in the sky,   As they go by,
The airplanes fly,   I will not cry.

70. Repeat the Sound (P)   (2 or more players)

Materials: List of sentences with words that repeat sounds.

Directions: Players make and read sentences with the same sound in them. Others are to identify the repeated sound.

Example: (1) The fat cat caught a rat. (2) Grab the cab and gab. (3) The crack in back of the shack sounded like a ticktack. (4) Dad was glad and not mad. (5) Shake and bake the cake.

II. STRUCTURAL ANALYSIS

A. INFLECTIONAL ENDINGS

71. Add-a-Step (P) (I)   (1 or more players)

Materials: List of root words and endings (s, es, ed, ing, y).

Directions: Players write root words and add endings to add a step at a time. Example:

j	u	m	p		
j	u	m	p	s	
j	u	m	p	e	d
j	u	m	p	i	n	g

Variation: Give a list of words to which endings have been added. Players are to underline root words.

72. Two of a Kind (P) (I)   (1 or more players)

Materials: List of root words and endings.

Directions: Players add two endings to the same root word and write a sentence using the newly formed words.

Variation: "What has been added?" Players underline the endings that have been added to the root words.

73. Today, Yesterday, Tomorrow (P) (I)   (1 or more players)

Materials: List of root words; paper and pencil for each player.

Directions: Players write Today, Yesterday, and Tomorrow at the top of their paper. They add necessary words and endings to show the root words in the three columns.

Example:	Today	Yesterday	Tomorrow
jump	I jump. I am jumping.	I jumped.	I will jump.
talk	I talk. I am talking.	I talked.	I will talk.

74. Compare and Draw (P) (I)   (2 or more players)

Materials: List of words, art paper, crayons.

Directions: The leader writes comparative words on the board, and players illustrate each word.

> big, bigger, biggest   wide, wider, widest
> tall, taller, tallest   slow, slower, slowest
> small, smaller, smallest   fast, faster, fastest
> cold, colder, coldest   fat, fatter, fattest

Variations: Players cut out pictures for each word, and paste them next to the word. Another variation is to supply pictures and words. Players match (or draw lines between) the words and pictures.

B. PLURALS

75. Fishing for Words (P) (I)   (1 or more players)

Materials: Words printed on fish-shaped cards; pole; line; small magnet. Words are printed on cards cut in the shape of fish, and scattered face down on the floor or in a bowl. Each fish has a paper clip or staples fastened to it. The small magnet is fastened to one end of a fishing line which should be attached to the pole.

Directions: Players take turns fishing for cards. As the magnet comes in contact with the metal on a "fish," it lifts from the floor or bowl. Players pronounce the word and give its plural form to keep the fish. The player catching the most fish wins.

Variations: Use phrases or sentences instead of words. Say the word and identify it as a singular or plural.

76. Plural Football (P) (I)   (2 or more players)

Materials: A set of word cards, a cardboard football, and a football field made of oaktag. On a large sheet of paper or oaktag, draw a football field with sections to represent ten yards each. The game begins at the 50-yard line, where the football is placed. The set of cards has a word or phrase on each card.

Directions: The first player or team reads the word or phrase on the first card and pronounces its plural form. If the player reads the word correctly, he moves the ball ten yards toward the opponent's goal. If the word is read incorrectly, the player has fumbled the ball, and it is moved 10 yards toward his own goal. The other player or team picks up a card and reads it. When a team or player crosses the goal line of the opponent, his score is six. If he reads the next word correctly, he receives an extra point. The player or team with the higher score wins. *See following illustration.*

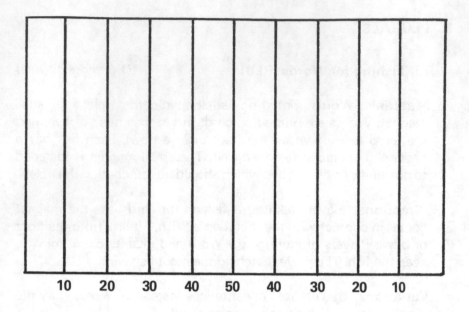

| 10 | 20 | 30 | 40 | 50 | 40 | 30 | 20 | 10 |

77. Postman Game (P) (I)   (2 or more players)

Materials: A class mailbox; plurals of words (one to a card), and envelopes.

Directions: Place a word on a card in an envelope. Give a different envelope to each player. A player must say the word and use it in a sentence. Then he may mail it in the mailbox.

Variations: Use sentences or phrases. Use pictures to show one or more than one.

Each player receives a "letter" from the postman and opens the envelope. The player opens the envelope, pronounces the word, and uses it in a sentence. If he does so correctly, he receives a point. If not, the letter is returned to the mailbox.

78. Wordo (P) (I)   (3 or more players)

Materials: Make "Wordo" cards (like Bingo), markers, words on small cards. (See Game No. 67.) Cards should contain words to be reviewed. The same word may appear on most of the cards but in different positions.

Directions: Players cover the words as they are called. The first player to cover five words horizontally, vertically, or diagonally says, "Wordo," and wins.

Variations: Use prefixes, suffixes, or initial consonants instead of review words.

C. ROOT WORDS

79. What's the Root Word? (P) (I)   (1 or more players)

Materials: Make a list of words with prefixes, suffixes, and other endings.

Directions: Players copy the words, underline the root word, and rewrite the root word. Examples: cutting, decided, baker, sunny, dresses, Tommy, giggle, biggest, cried.

Variation: Make two sets of cards. On one set, write root words; on the other set, put the same words with prefixes and suffixes. Players match the longer word with the root word.

80. Find the Root Word (P) (I)   (2 or more players)

Materials: List of words containing prefixes, suffixes, and endings—written on cards.

Directions: A player picks a card from the pile and answers the following questions:

1. What is the word?   2. What is the root word?   3. What has been added?   4. How has the prefix, suffix or ending changed the meaning of the root word? Players score one point for each correct answer.

81. End It Yourself (P) (I)   (1 or more players)

Materials: List of three-letter combinations.

Directions: A player is given a three-letter combination. He completes the word, using as many letters as possible. One point is allowed for each letter used.

Examples: som - some (1 point)   tha - thanks (3 points)
                  somebody (5 points)   thanksgiving (9 points)

        lif - life (1 point)   fol - fold (1 point)
              lift (1 point)   followers (6 points)

82. Surprise Game (P)   (1 or more players)

Materials: Words with endings written on cards.

Directions: Cards are placed face down. Each player, in turn, takes a surprise. If he can say the word, he may keep the surprise. If he cannot pronounce the word, he must return the card. The player with the most cards (surprises) wins.

83. Look and Clap Game (P)   (2 or more players)

Materials: Word cards for the leader.

Directions: New words to be learned are on word cards. Players must watch the cards as the leader flashes each card. Players clap their hands when they see a new word.

84. Be a Word Builder (P) (I)   (1 or more players)

Materials: List of root words, paper and pencil for each player.

Directions: Players form as many new words as they can by adding an ending (s, es, ed, ing, y). The player with the most correct words wins. Example: jump, jumps, jumped, jumping, jumpy.

Variations: Players add prefixes to words; suffixes to words.

D. COMPOUND WORDS

85. Split the Words (P) (I)   (1 or more players)

Materials: List of compound words for each player.

Directions: Players must split the compound words into two smaller words. One point is allowed for each correct answer.

Examples:

everything	someone	firewood
suppertime	bedroom	butterfly
barnyard	cannot	spacesuit
cornfield	somewhere	bluebird

86. Make Compound Words (P) (I)   (1 or more players)

Materials: Compound words written on cards. Cut the words into two parts.

Directions: Word cards are mixed and placed on a desk. Players arrange words to make compound words.

Variation: Groups of words are listed on paper. Players combine words in one column with those in a second column, by drawing a line between the two short words to make a compound word. Examples:

after	green	air	fish
bare	way	base	room
church	noon	class	town
door	yard	down	ball
ever	foot	gold	plane

87. Big and Little (P)　　　　(1 or more players or teams)

Materials: 2 word wheels, 2 spinners, 32 word cards.

Directions: After cards are separated, use a paper fastener to hold each spinner on a wheel. Place the cards face up. Players take turns spinning for compound words. They use one word wheel and then the other. As a player spins a word, he takes a matching card. When both spins are completed, the two cards are put together to see if they form a compound word. Two points are allowed for each compound word. If no compound word is formed after two spins, no points are allowed. The player or team with the most points wins the game.

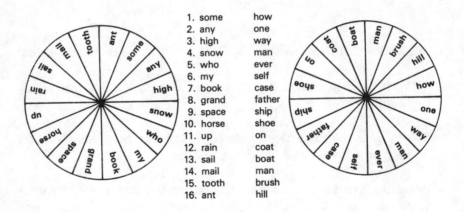

1. some	how
2. any	one
3. high	way
4. snow	man
5. who	ever
6. my	self
7. book	case
8. grand	father
9. space	ship
10. horse	shoe
11. up	on
12. rain	coat
13. sail	boat
14. mail	man
15. tooth	brush
16. ant	hill

E. CONTRACTIONS

88. Rewrite Contractions (P) (I)   (1 or more players)

Materials: List of contractions.

Directions: Players are given a list of contractions to rewrite the two words that each contraction represents. The player with the largest number correct wins. Examples:

I'll   you'll   I'm   they've   you'd   she's   don't

89. Contracto (P) (I)   (1 or more players)

Materials: List of words that can be changed into contractions.

Directions: A player reads the list and rewrites each pair of words into a contraction. Examples: you will, I will, you should, have not, it will, you are, you would, you will, do not, I have, they will, I am.

F. REVERSALS

90. Trace and Sound Out (P) (I)   (1 or more players)

Materials: List of reversals with which players have difficulty.

Directions: A player traces over words with which he is having difficulty. As he traces over each letter, he makes the sound of that letter for as long as it takes him to write it. Both sound and tracing should be even. Encourage players to blend the sound of one letter into the next. Common reversals:

was	saw	eat	tea	dear	read
war	raw	pets	step	left	felt
stop	spot	gum	mug	team	meat
nets	nest	on	no	board	broad
dog	god	won	now	slate	stale
dig	big	top	pot	least	steal
then	when	there	where	but	tub

91. Stop and Go (P) (I)   (1 or more players)

Materials: On green and red paper, make phrase cards with reversals. Make fewer red cards than green cards.

Directions: Players read all green cards aloud, but must stop reading aloud the red cards. They are read silently.

Examples: in the steps of pets   on the no
                into saw and was   in eat and tea

Variation: Prepare sentences with the common reversals and have players read the sentences. Players receive one point for each reversal read correctly. Examples:

(1) The **pot** was on the **top** of the table. (2) He will **stop** on this **spot** . (3) He has **now won** the prize. (4) **Dig** a **big** hole.

G. SYLLABLES

92. Countdown (P) (I)   (2 or more players)

Materials: Draw a rocket game with 10 lines on each side (see below); list of syllables.

Directions: From the list of syllables, each player makes a word and writes it on his side of the rocket. Syllables may be used more than once, but players may not use the same word twice or use a word of the other player. The first player to countdown 10-1 wins.

10	mid	so	pen	ap
9	bot	pi	sum	fun
8	lem	no	sim	sal
7	per	gar	de	cir
6	be	teach	mer	cus
5	da	side	den	tice
4	ad	ple	son	tle
3	ny	er	lot	dle
2	cil	cide	on	an
1	ly	ing	re	dis

93. Cut the Syllable (P) (I)   (1 or more players)

Materials: Words on cards; scissors.

Directions: With scissors, players cut words into syllables.

Examples:			
children	butter	farming	happy
before	invite	spelling	dinner
began	weekly	friendly	sister

Variation: Players look in a book to find (a) 5 words of one syllable (b) 5 words of two syllables (c) 5 words of three syllables.

94. Clap the Syllable (P) (2 or more players)

Materials: List of words with more than one syllable.

Directions: Players look at each word and clap the number of syllables in each word as they pronounce the word. Players score two points for each correct word—one point for clapping the word correctly, and one point for the correct pronunciation. The player with the most points wins.

95. Search for Syllables (P) (I) (2 or more players)

Materials: List of words with (1) prefixes (2) suffixes; paper and pencil for each player.

Directions: Players race to see who can underline the syllables correctly in each word. Examples:

retell	incorrect	lovely	useless
unopened	dislike	sadness	restful

H. PREFIXES AND SUFFIXES

96. Dominoes (I) (1 or more players)

Materials: Make dominoes on 3 X 5" cards (with roots, prefixes, and suffixes). Some dominoes will have root words on both ends and the other dominoes with the suffix on the first part and a prefix on the second part.

Directions: Players match the dominoes to add a prefix or a suffix to each word.

Examples:

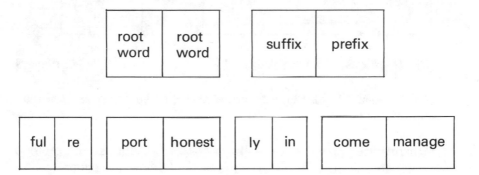

97. Prefix-Suffix Bingo (I) (2 or more players)

Materials: Bingo cards with root words across the top; prefixes and suffixes across the bottom.

Directions: Place five root words across the top of each card. In the squares below, write a prefix, suffix, or both. If the word "report" is called by the leader, players look under "port" and cover "re." If "reporter" is called, players look under "port" and cover the square with "re" and "er." The winner is the first player to cover five squares horizontally, vertically, or diagonally. *See following illustration.*

Prefix-Suffix Bingo

port	test	arm	rest	vent
de-	re-	dis-	-ful	ad-
de- ment	ing	un- -ed	un-	-less
-er	-ed	FREE	-ed	con-
re-	-er	-y	-less	in-
sup-	de- -able	-ful	-ing	pre- -ed

98. Prefix-Suffix Checkers (I) (2 players)

Materials: Checkerboard with a prefix or suffix in each square; set of checkers.

Directions: Play the game like checkers, except use the prefix or suffix in a word before you move a checker into the square.

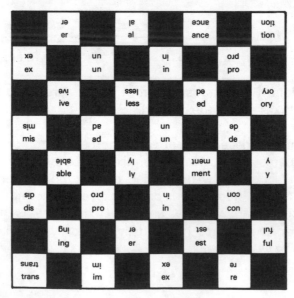

I. POSSESSIVES

99. Where Does It Go? (P) (I)   (1 or more players)

Materials: List of possessive words; pencil and paper for each player.

Directions: Players make four columns on their paper, and write in each column the singular, the possessive singular, the plural and the possessive plural of each word. Apostrophes should be placed correctly.

Singular	Possessive	Plural	Possessive
boy	boy's	boys	boys'
policeman	policeman's	policemen	policemen's
baby	baby's	babies	babies'
fox	fox's	foxes	foxes'
city	city's	cities	cities'
lady	lady's	ladies	ladies'

100. Whose? (P)   (2 or more players)

Materials: Sentences with possessives.

Directions: Players read the sentences, and tell to whom something belongs. Examples: This is Larry's book. "My dog is brown," said Jack. The baby's rattle is red.

III. WORD MEANING AND COMPREHENSION

A. PICTURE CLUES TO MEANING

101. Picture Card Fun (P) (2 or more players)

Materials: Make a set of picture cards and divide them between the players. On each card, paste a picture or draw a picture word and three words—one identifying the picture.

Directions: Players take turns flashing the picture cards for one another. The players must use the word in a sentence. One point is allowed for identifying the correct word label, and one point for using the word correctly in a sentence. The player who scores the most points wins.

102. Word-Picture Games (P) (I) (1 or more players)

Materials: Supply a sheet or card with phrases for each player.

Directions: A player finishes each phrase by adding one or two words from the list—to give a clearer word picture.

cold	rainy	1. a_____ _____morning
tall	green-eyed	2. a_____ _____boy
red	wooden	3. the _____ _____door
rocky	sandy	4. the_____ _____shore
old	hunter's	5. a_____ _____cabin

B. CONTEXT CLUES

103. Definition Clues (I)   (1 or more players)

Materials: Make a list of sentences (on a card, sheet, or chalk-board) in which an unknown word is defined in a sentence, and the definition given as a clue (see below). Provide words, if necessary for spelling.

Directions: A player reads and completes the sentences as fast as he or she can.

1. Willy is the world's largest animal.
   He is a large, swimming _____.   stars
2. Our flag has fifty of them. They are
   white, five-pointed _____.   whale
3. Jim was one of the men who landed on
   the moon. He is called an _____.   spaghetti
4. Look at the pretty red flower.
   The thorns on the stem protect
   the sweet-smelling _____.   astronaut
5. I like meatballs and tomato sauce with
   my favorite food, which is long, thin
   _____.   rose

104. Conductor-Reading Game (P)   (5 or more players)

Materials: A set of flash cards with vocabulary words.

Directions: One player acts as conductor. The other players sit in a semi-circle. The conductor stands behind the first seated player. The teacher or leader flashes a word card. The player who answers first by identifying the word, moves and stands behind the second-seated player, and another card is flashed to continue the game.

105. Experience Clues (P) (I) (1 or more players)

Materials: Make a list of sentences (on card, sheet, or chalkboard) in which an unknown word makes sense in terms of a player's own experience.

Directions: A player reads and completes the sentences as fast as she or he can.

1. The butcher sliced the ham with a___.	flowers
2. The bride carried a large bouquet of___.	records
3. The lady put a dry___on her crying baby.	knife
4. He knocked on the door of the old brick ___.	diaper
5. She played two new___on my phonograph.	building

106. Put Them Together (I) (1 or more players)

Materials: Mark three envelopes—one labeled N, another V, and the third one O. In the N envelope, place individual printed phrases which are noun phrases; in the V envelope, place the same number of verb phrases; in the O envelope, do the same with objective phrases.

Directions: In turn, a player chooses from the N envelope, the next player from the V envelope, and a third player from the O envelope. Players work together and read the sentence they have formed.

N	V	O
a turkey	made faces	with a goose
two mice	laughed	with a dog
a tulip	danced	at the elephant
three fleas	ran off	at the monkey
a clown	dried up	at the market

Variation: Players can add their own phrases to each envelope.

(1 or more players)

h space for drawing.

ture to complete each sentence

(1 or more players)

rds and definition for each.

cramble the words on the chalk-
 she or he can.

d u n o s (noise)
t a t o o p (vegetable)
m o n a w (a lady)

ld scrambled words and defini-

(2 or more players or teams)

Materials: List of scrambled sentences in two columns on the chalkboard (or on 2 cards).

Handwritten notes:

Pai

vocabulary build-up 244
p. 145 - writes a word as
many ways as can -syn.

common language 227
p. 138 expressions

) similes for sentences 217
p. 132

) create metaphors 219
p. 133

) find the mistake 148
p. 96

) unscramble words 108, 137
p. 79, 91

) end it yourself 81
p. 65 3 letter combos

) word pyramids 46
p. 47 start w/ 1 vowel

Directions: Divide the group into teams. Each team unscrambles the sentences in one column. The first to finish wins.

1. landed my piano fly on
2. cat lion a the roared little like
3. in caught the a was web fly spider
4. smell flowers sweet some
5. rowed river lady the down the

Variation: Have each player add to the list.

110. Word Association (P) (I)   (2 or more players or teams)

Materials: List of prepositions and list of adjectives for a player or team.

Directions: A player or team suggests other words which can be associated with the following: (Example: **over** the rainbow; **cool** evening).

Prepositions:	across	before	on	through
	above	down	to	behind
	after	inside	by	beside
Adjectives:	red	happy	tiny	dry
	best	cold	long	wet
	green	dark	warm	black

Variations: Have pupils add to the list.

111. Comparison or Contrast Clues (I)   (1 or more players)

Materials: Make a list of sentences in which an unknown word may be used because it is evident in contrast or comparison.

Directions: A player reads and completes each sentence as fast as she or he can.

1. A rabbit has a short tail, but a squirrel has a___tail.
2. Birds and planes have___to fly.
3. Roses are red, but violets are___.
4. Betty likes to jump up and___.
5. The moon is a round___in the night sky.

112. Riddle Clues (P)   (1 or more players or teams)

Materials: Make a list of riddles for each player or team.

Directions: A player or team tries to solve the riddles before the other player or team does.

1. I got a birthday present. I can read it. What is it?
2. I sang it, and John played it on the piano? What is it?
3. These birds honk and migrate. What are they?

113. Familiar Expression Clues (I)   (1 or more players)

Materials: Make a list of sentences in which an unknown word is supplied because it fits naturally into a cliche that is familiar.

Directions: Same as for previous game above.

1. Popcorn is as white as___.
2. Jack is as stubborn as a___.
3. She sat as quiet as a___.
4. My toes feel as cold as___.
5. I feel as warm as___.

114. Reflection of Mood (P) (I)   (1 or more players or teams)

Materials: List of sentences for each player.

Directions: A player decides (as fast as she or he can) how someone or something might feel.
1. Margaret lost her purse. She cried. She felt ___.
2. Tim ate 6 apples. He couldn't eat another bite. Tim felt ___.
3. Bob kicked the can, yelled at the dog, and slammed the door. Bob felt ___.
4. Sue's knees knocked as she walked slowly up the squeaky dark stairway. Sue felt ___.
5. The cat drank a warm dish of milk and curled up on a soft cushion. The cat seemed ___.

115. Story Starters (P) (I)   (1 or more players or teams)

Materials: Write unfinished sentences on the chalkboard.

Directions: A player or team selects and finishes a sentence. They can develop the idea by telling more about the experience.
1. I feel lazy today because ___.
2. I can't drive a boat, but ___.
3. Playing at the seashore is fun because ___.
4. I can't go out to play today because ___.
5. Watching my favorite TV program is fun because ___.

116. Character's Emotion (I)   (1 or more players)

Materials: Choose a story (or stories) in which a character's mood or feelings change in the course of the action.

Directions: Players complete sentences, providing the **when** and **wherefore,** referring to the story as needed.

1. Dick was excited when___.
2. Dick was unhappy when his flashlight went out because___.
3. He was puzzled when___.

117. How Do They Feel? (P) (I)   (1 or more players or teams)

Materials: Display an action picture from a magazine or newspaper.

Directions: Players tell **what** they think is happening, **how** they think each character feels, and **why** they think the characters feel as they do.

Variations: Extend the game by having individuals supply probable conversation.

118. Make It Up—Fill It In (I)   (1 or more players)

Materials: Sheet of paper and pencil for each player.

Directions: Each player makes up and writes a set of sentences, omitting one word in each sentence. A pair of players exchanges papers and fills in appropriate words in each other's sentences. When papers are returned, they can be discussed to show why certain context clues worked, and why some may not have worked.

Example: Chipmunks like to climb_____.

Variation: For primary groups, use multiple-choice sentences instead of completion. (Example: Jill likes to play—cat, ball, draw.)

C. CLASSIFICATION—RELATIONSHIPS

119. Which Doesn't Belong? (P)   (1 or more players)

Materials: Make cards with word groups, one of which doesn't belong.

Directions: A player draws a line through the word which does not belong in the same classification.

1. buildings: house, barn, hotel, road
2. clothing: shirt, scarf, book, shoes
3. flowers: tulip, carrot, rose, daisy
4. vegetables: peas, corn, jelly, celery

120. What Is It? (P)   (1 or more players)

Materials: Write sentences for each player.

Directions: A player copies each sentence, crossing out the two wrong answers.

1. An evil thing is long, good, bad.
2. A wagon has one, four, three wheels.
3. An oak is a tree, bicycle, flower.

121. Which? (P) (I)   (1 or more players)

Materials: List of sentences and words.

Directions: A player copies the sentences and writes each correct answer.

1. Which are children?	girl	boy	mother
2. Which are pets?	dog	cat	rocket
3. Which can walk?	horse	house	chicken
1. Which pollute?	smoke	air	trash
2. Which is a doctor?	pediatrician	philatelist	graphologist
3. Which is a space station?	Apollo	Skylab	Saturn

122. Add a Word (P) (I)   (1 or more players)

Materials: On cards, write words that are related, and a second list of words for players to fill in.

Directions: Players copy the related words and add a word from the list (at right) that goes with those at left.

milk, bread, eggs,_____ six
one, four, seven_____ sheep
pig, cow, horse, _____ Mary
Perry, Pat Wendy_____ cake

123. Seeing Relationships (P) (I)   (1 or more players)

Materials: Pairs of word cards or picture cards.

Directions: A player matches word or picture cards that are related. Players tell how their matching cards are related.

shoe—stocking	bread—jelly	log—ax
pancake—syrup	cup—saucer	pillow—blanket

124. What Can You Do With It?   (2 or more players)

Materials: Word cards.

Directions: A leader writes the title of the game on the chalk-board, and flashes word cards to elicit answers from the players.

knife	water	stove	bed	rug
apple	egg	stairs	chair	scarf
rocket	coat	glasses	dog	toothbrush

125. What's It For? (P)   (1 or more players)

Materials: Make a list of words and a multiple-choice group of answers.

Directions: Players read the words at left and then circle the words (at right) that tell what you do with the object.

1. chair   read it—play it—sit on it
2. slacks   hear them—wear them—color them
3. plane   eat it—ride it—comb it
4. tulip   smell it—cook it—freeze it
5. lake   sleep in it—swim in it—drink it

126. What Would You Need? (P)   (1 or more players)

Materials: List of questions and words.

Directions: Players use the following words to answer this question: What would you need to___? and then volunteer answers.

ride	eat	sleep	splash
dance	smell	run	paint
see	drink	write	ski

127. Barnyard Frolic (P) (3 or more players)

Materials: Two sets of cards with the name of a farm animal on one card in each set (duck, horse, cow). Print the word Barnyard on one of the cards. The leader keeps one set of cards and distributes the other set to players.

Directions: The leader holds up a card with the word **duck** on it. The player with the matching card quacks like a duck. When the leader holds up the **Barnyard** card, all players respond with the typical sound made by the animal on his or her card.

128. Headings and Words (I) (1 or more players)

Materials: Provide a sheet with headings and a group of words.

Directions: A player lists the words under the proper headings.
TRANSPORTATION   COMMUNICATION

satellite, rocket
radar, submarine
newspaper, TV
rail, highway
transmitter, radio

D. SYNONYMS AND ANTONYMS

129. Circle Game (P) (I)   (3 or more players)

Materials: Word cards with synonyms.

Directions: Players sit in a circle. Word cards are placed face down in the center. In turn, players pick up a card, read the word, and give a synonym for it. If a player is correct, he keeps the card. Otherwise, it is placed at the center (face down). The player with most cards wins the game.

130. Take Your Pick (P)   (1 or more players)

Materials: Cards with lines of words.

Directions: A player underlines the word which means the same or nearly the same as the first word in each line.

1. shiny   few — high — bright
2. bag   bushel — box — sack
3. false   wrong — odd — ship

Variation: Provide the same type of cards, but use antonyms.

131. Ladder Game (P) (1 or more players)

Materials: A card with two extremes or opposites to build from one to the other (see below).

Directions: A player writes words in the ladder to show differences between antonyms.

Example: hot—warm—cool—cold.

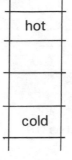

132. Words That Mean the Same (P) (I) (1 or more players)

Materials: List of words for a matching game.

Directions: A player draws a line between synonymous words.

1. tall	happy	5. cabin	under
2. fast	above	6. below	late
3. joyful	quick	7. tardy	sleepy
4. cover	high	8. tired	hut

133. Paired Words (I) (1 or more players)

Materials: List of paired words—some synonyms and some antonyms for each player.

Directions: A player writes "S" between each pair of synonyms, and "A" between each pair of antonyms.

1. modern____ancient   4. decrease____increase
2. govern____rule   5. speak____orate
3. middle____center   6. supply____provide

134. Two for One (I)   (1 or more players)

Materials: List of words that have a synonym and an atnonym.

Directions: A player writes a synonym and an antonym for each word.

1. anger _____ _____   2. decrease _____ _____
3. lively _____ _____   4. noisy _____ _____
5. smart _____ _____   6. thoughtful _____ _____

135. Opposites (P) (I)   (1 or more players)

Materials: List of words.

Directions: Players read each word and suggest an opposite.

1. little   1. stop   1. laughed
2. walk   2. white   2. idle
3. yes   3. out   3. reliable
4. he   4. on   4. angry
5. girl   5. down   5. located

136. Guessing Opposites (P)   (1 or more players)

Materials: List of incomplete sentences.

Directions: A player writes in the missing word in each sentence.

1. Sugar is sweet, but vinegar is____.
2. Airplanes move fast, but turtles are____.
3. The ground is below, and the sky is____.

137. Unscramble the Word (P) (I)   (1 or more players)

Materials: On the chalkboard, list words in scrambled order. Besides each scrambled word, write a clue or definition that is a synonym or antonym.

Directions: Players use the clues to unscramble the words.
1. c i r e e v e   (opposite of transmit)
2. e e m m r r b e   (same as recall)
3. g r e d a r   (same as concern)
4. y i l e l k   (opposite of unlikely)

E. WORDS WITH MULTIPLE MEANINGS

138. What Does It Mean? (P)   (1 or more players)

Materials: Make cards with words, sentences, and multiple meanings.

Directions: A player reads each word and its two meanings. Then he writes the correct number above each <u>underlined</u> word in the sentence to show which meaning it has.

---

fall   (1) a time of year   (2) drop

---

1. In **fall**, we get ready for winter.
2. Watch out, or you will **fall**.
3. Did the rain **fall** yesterday?

139. Meaning and Function Words (P) (I)   (1 or more players)

Materials: On the chalkboard, write words with multiple meanings.

Directions: Players use the words in sentences to show the different meanings each word has.

Examples: bat, fly, right, club, building, show.

140. Multiple Meanings (I)   (1 or more players)

Materials: Sheet of paper with instructions, meanings, and sentences.

Directions: A player reads the directions and indicates his answers by writing the correct letter of the meaning that tells how the word is used in the sentence.

---

right: (a) correct   (b) opposite of left   (c) good or lawful

---

1. Under the law, you did the <u>right</u> thing.
2. Did you give the <u>right</u> answer?
3. Turn <u>right</u> at the next corner.
4. Are you on the <u>right</u> page?

Variation: Have players supply their own sentences.

141. One-in-Three (P)   (1 or more players)

Materials: Cards with words and meanings to choose from.

Directions: A player draws a line from each word to its correct meaning.

1. cane   a chair   2. barn   a tower
          a walking stick   a motel
          a sweater   a stable

3. ram   a goat   4. cravat a belt
          a cat   a tie
          a stick   a knot

F. HONONYMS

142. Say It — Spell It (P) (I)   (groups or teams)

Materials: List of homonyms for the leader.

Directions: The leader pronounces a homonym. In turn, a team member spells the word and uses it in a sentence (for 2 points). If a member of the same team gives the second spelling, and uses it correctly in a sentence, three points are scored.

bear—bare	pear—pair	which—witch
cell—sell	tied—tide	peace—piece
beat—beet	bore—boar	where—wear
red—read	lead—led	fare—fair
rode—road	great—grate	some—sum

143. Circle One (P)   (1 or more players)

Materials: List of sentences with underlined homonyms.

Directions: A player circles the correct homonym in each sentence.

1. I'd like a big **peace piece** of cake.
2. Add the numbers to find the **sum some**.
3. I **knew new** the answer to the question.

144. You Decide (I)   (1 or more players)

Materials: List of homonyms for each player.

Directions: A player writes a sentence to show the meaning of each homonym.

site: _____

sight:

week: _____

weak:

G. STRUCTURAL WORDS AND PHRASES

145. Spin and Match (P)   (2 or more players or teams)

Materials: 2 word wheels, 32 cards from Game No. 87.

Directions: Spin for short words to recognize and match. Players take turns to spin a word. They find the matching word card and pronounce the word. Two points are awarded for each word matched and pronounced. Otherwise, cards are returned to the table, and no points are awarded.
Note: 2 or more persons or teams can play with one word wheel and matching cards at the same time.

146. Choose the Correct Words (P) (I)   (1 or more players)

Materials: Phrases written on the chalkboard; paper with incompleted sentences, and pencil for each player.

Directions: Players write the number of the phrase to complete each unfinished sentence.

Chalkboard: 1. something in a city 2. something to eat
                    3. something to play

Paper: A taxi is___.   A wagon is___.
                   A store is___.   A banana is___.
                   A doll is___.   Cookies are___.

147. What Do I Do? (P) (1 or more players)

Materials: Make a card with incomplete sentences, and a list of words.

Directions: Players copy the incomplete sentences but add a word to finish each sentence.

1. We____with our ears.   work
2. We____with our eyes.   hear
3. We____with our hands.   chew
4. We____with our feet.   dance
5. We____with our teeth.   see

148. Find the Mistake (P) (I) (1 or more players)

Materials: Write sentences on a card and include a mistake in each sentence.

Directions: Players find each error, draw a line through it, and write in correct words or phrases.

1. The motel was a short distant away from our house.
2. We watching TV on Mary's house.
3. Everyone expect I is going to the game.

149. Which Phrase? (P) (I)   (1 or more players)

Materials: List of words and phrases.

Directions: A player puts the words and phrases together to make a complete sentence.

1. The hay is	over the moon.
2. The cow jumped	in a squeaky voice.
3. The mouse spoke	in the barn.
4. The clown slipped	above the clouds.
5. The plane flew	on the ice.

150. Total Sentence Meaning (P) (I)   (1 or more players)

Materials: Card with list of sentences containing an unnecessary word or phrase.

Directions: Players write the sentence, omitting the word or phrase that doesn't belong.

1. Gene can ride with with us.
2. Come along to the to the circus.
3. Did you hear the news new?

H. READING FOR DETAILS

151. Name the Title (P) (I)   (group)

Materials: none.

Directions: The group of players sits in a circle or row. The leader calls out the name of a character in a book which the group has read. The leader hands an eraser (or some small object) to one player. If that player can give the title of the book in which the character appears (before the leader counts silently to 10) the player wins a point. If he or she cannot answer correctly, the player becomes "it."

152. How? When? Where? (P) (I)   (1 or more players)

Materials: Three headings (How? When? Where?) across the top of a sheet of paper; word and phrase cards to answer the questions.

Directions: A player places each word or phrase card under the correct heading, as fast as he or she can.

into a room	every day	slow
with a bang	at last	in his house
in the yard	everywhere	over the hill

153. Twenty Questions (P) (I)   (group or teams)

Materials: Book of stories, with contents.

Directions: Players check the titles in the Table of Contents to remember them. One player leaves the room while the other players select a title. Then the player comes back into the room and asks as many as 20 questions, which can be answered with a yes or no answer to help determine which title was chosen. Allow five points for each correct answer.

154. Who — What — When — Where — How or Why? (P) (I)
(1 or more players)

Materials: A set of cards, each with a short story that contains answers to the title questions.

Directions: On a separate sheet of paper, a player writes the questions on separate lines. He reads the story and writes the answer after each question.

Peter went fishing this morning. He had his fishing pole and bait ready the night before. Peter went to Long Pond because he knew the fishing was good, and it was a good place to meet other fisherman. Fishing is one of Peter's hobbies.

155. Following Directions (P) (I)
(1 or more players)

Materials: Fold a half sheet of easel paper into eight squares. Number the squares.

Directions: A player does what the directions "tell" him to do in the corresponding square.

1. Write 5 things seen on a farm.
2. Write 4 things in a hospital.
3. Write 6 things at a zoo.
4. Write 3 things at the beach.
5. Write 8 things in a market.
6. Write 3 things done at school.
7. Write 3 things in the sky.
8. Write 5 things about yourself.

156. Do As It Says (P)   (pairs of players)

Materials: Cards with specific details or directions.

Directions: A pair of players uses the same information card. One player physically does what the card says; the second player checks to see that directions are followed exactly.

Stand up and walk to the nearest window in the room. Count three things you see out the window. Come back and tell your partner what you have seen. Sit in your seat. Salute your partner.

157. Make What It Says (P)   (1 or more players)

Materials: Individual directions printed on cards; colored papers; scissors.

Directions: A player makes what the directions say. The player cuts out the object(s) mentioned in the directions.

1. a white house   2. a green umbrella
3. a yellow boat   4. a red flower

158. Read, Draw, and Color (P)   (1 or more players)

Materials: Directions on the chalkboard; drawing paper and crayons.

Directions: A player reads the directions, then draws and colors what the directions say.

1. Draw 2 puppies. Color one black and one brown.
2. Draw a red, yellow, and blue ball.
3. Draw a car. Color it green. Draw a truck. Color it red.

159. Color the Balloons (P)   (1 or more players)

Materials: A chalkboard drawing of 8 balloons and a list of key words.

Directions: Players draw 8 balloons like those on the board, but omit the number. Instead, the players color the balloons according to the number key.

KEY: 1. blue
2. green
3. red
4. yellow
5. brown
6. orange
7. black
8. purple

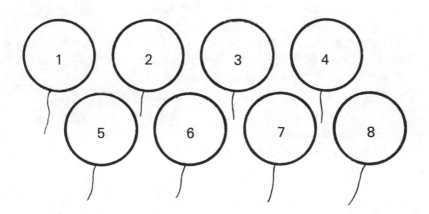

160. Do You Remember? (P) (I)   (1 or more players)

Materials: Story cards with questions and multiple-choice answers.

Directions: A player reads the story and questions. Then he circles his choice of answers.

An alley cat caught a mouse and held it by the tail.
1. Who caught the mouse?
2. How was the mouse held?

Variation: For more able pupils, you might add more details and questions.

161. Who Am I? (P) (I)   (2 or more players)

Materials: Paper and pencil for each player.

Directions: Each player writes a list of clues about a familiar story character. Players exchange papers and try to guess the character with as few clues as possible.

1. She wasn't married   2. She was small.
3. She was eating.   4. A spider sat beside her.
5. She was frightened.   6. She sat on a tuffet.
7. She was eating curds and whey.

IV. ORGANIZATION

A. CLASSIFYING WORDS AND INFORMATION

162. Organization Game (P)   (1 or more players)

Materials: List of picture words, paper and pencil or crayons.

Directions: Each player copies the names of things that grow, and draws a picture next to each name.

a tree	a truck	a boy	a ball
a flower	a skyscraper	a girl	a bird
a house	a highway	a fish	a museum

Variation: Use other categories as months of the year, foods, numbers, clothing, animals, family members, holidays.

163. Animal, Vegetable, or Mineral? (P)   (2 or more players)

Materials: List of clues.

Directions: A player or leader calls out clues. The other players listen to the clue and try to guess the answers.

I am thinking of a word. It has six letters. It is a vegetable.
I am thinking of a word. It has five letters. It is a mineral.
I am thinking of a word. It has three letters. It is an animal.

164. Eat, Wear, or Ride It? (P) (2 or more players)

Materials: Each player makes three cards saying: eat, wear, ride. On the chalkboard or orally, give a list of words.

Directions: Each player raises the correct card in response to each word on the list (or given orally).

hat—shoes—orange—pie—car—horse—meat—ice cream
skirt—scarf—tomato—train—space capsule—wagon

165. Classifying Words (P) (2 or more players or teams)

Materials: List of about 10 nouns written on the chalkboard; sheet of paper and pencil for each player. The sheets are divided into fifths and headings are added: SEE, HEAR, FEEL, TASTE, SMELL.

Directions: Each player or team writes each of the words under the proper heading:

box—chocolate—wind—rain—snow—flowers—yell—plane
pie—goat—garden (add any words in players' reading
vocabulary)

B. SEQUENCE

166. Sequence Drawings (P)   (1 or more players)

Materials: Comic strips cut into 3 or more panels.

Directions: A player looks at the panels of a comic-strip story, and arranges them in proper sequence as to time or events.

167. Watching for Sequence (P) (I)   (individual)

Materials: Card with sentences out of sequence; paper and pencil for each player.

Directions: A player reads the sentences, and writes 1, 2, or 3 in front of each sentence to show the order in which the story happened.

_____ James gave a button to a squirrel.

_____ The squirrel chattered.

_____ James went for a walk and met a squirrel.

A player numbers each sentence to show what happens when you hunt giant earthworms:

_____ Dig into burrows until you find one with enough worm exposed.

_____ Listen to the giant earthworms near the surface of the ground.

_____ Ease the worm out of its burrow — inch by inch.

_____ Keep digging and follow the twisting burrow to avoid breaking the worm.

_____ Tie a knot into the exposed part of the worm.

168. Put Them in Order (P)   (1 or more players)

Materials: Wall chart with story events in incorrect order.

Directions: A player arranges sentences in the wall chart in the order in which the events took place in a story.

169. What We Did and When (P)   (group)

Materials: Chalk and board; paper and pencil for each player.

Directions: Players volunteer things they did during a particular day. List them on the chalkboard. Each player must arrange the sentences in the order of happening.

170. Can You Remember? (P) (I)   (2 or more players)

Materials: Book for each player.

Directions: Each player brings a book to the game. When it is a player's turn to give a report, he or she designates a page he or she will read to the group. After reading, the other players ask questions which bring out what happened before and after the incident read.

171. Supposing (P) (1 or more players)

Materials: List of sentences and questions (see below).

Directions: A player decides which would be done first in a sequence of two actions.

1. Suppose you wanted to eat a soft-boiled egg. Which would you do first—put salt on the egg, or peel the shell?
2. Suppose you wanted to go to the store. Which would you do first—go into the store, or pick out what you want to buy?

172. Make a Story (P) (individual)

Materials: Sentences of a story divided into strips and placed into an envelope.

Directions: A player arranges the sentence strips in proper sequence to make a story.

C. MAIN IDEAS

173. Name the Title (P) (I) (2 or more players)

Materials: none.

Directions: The players may be seated in a circle or row. The leader calls out the name of a book or story character with which the group is familiar. The leader points to one player who gives the title of the book that fits the character mentioned (before the leader can count to 10). If the player does so, he becomes a winner; if not, he becomes "it."

174. What's the Big Idea? (P) (1 or more players)

Materials: A card for each player (short story and possible answers).

Directions: A player reads the story and then checks the best title for the story:

In some zoos, there are animal helpers. They feed and care for new-born animals. Sometimes, the animal helpers take the young animals home with them until the young ones can take care of themselves.

Check the best title for this story:

____ Animal Homes ____ Animal Helpers

175. Find the Main Idea (I)   (individual)

Materials: A card for each player (short story and possible answers).

Directions: A player reads the story and then underlines the best title for the story (and both paragraphs).

NEW HOMES FROM TIRES

People are using old tires to make underwater homes for some fish. First, the tires are pressed into bundles by machine. The bundles are then tied with wire and dropped into the sea.

Fish swim to the tires and make homes there. The homes are safe for the fish and their young. Other tiny sea animals come to the tires and become food for the fish.

Read the titles below. Underline the best title for paragraph 1 of the story:
1. Tires and Wires in the Sea
2. How Tires Become Fish Homes
3. How People Use Old Tires

Underline the best title for paragraph 2:
1. Why Tires Make Good Fish Homes
2. Tires and Food
3. Fish Make Tire Homes

D. LISTING

176. Make a List (P)   (1 or more players)

Materials: Make cards with stories and directions for follow-up.

Directions: A player reads the story and then writes her or his answers.

Jane went for a walk through the woods. She saw an owl chasing a mouse. Just then, an eagle flew near, and the owl went away. When Jane got home she was glad to see that her pet dog and cat got along well.

Write the names of four animals mentioned in the story.
1. _____ (through 5)

177. Listing Facts (I)   (1 or more players)

Materials: A card with a story on it for each player, and directions.

Directions: Each player reads the story and then follows the directions.

The Skylab mission began with the blasting off of an unmanned Saturn V. The Skylab consists of the workshop, a telescope mount, an airlock module, and multiple docking adapter.
Twenty-four hours later, the first astronaut crew was launched in an Apollo module to rendezvous with the workshop. The first visit lasted 28 days.

Write the names of four things that will be part of Skylab.

E. SUMMARIZING

178. A Bird's Eye View (P) (I) (group)

Materials: Read a story to the group, or have players read a story.

Directions: Each player illustrates or provides answers to the following:

1. What is the name of the story?
2. Where does the story take place?
3. Who is in the story?
4. When does the story take place?

Some players may be able to show or tell the major events of the story.

F. SKIMMING

179. Zip Through (I)   (1 or more players)

Materials: Story card with questions for each player.

Directions: A player reads the story and then writes answers to the questions within a limited time set by the teacher or leader.

G. OUTLINING

180. One-Step Outline (I)   (1 or more players)

Materials: A story card and directions for each player.

Directions: Each player reads every paragraph in the story, and writes the main idea of each paragraph. A player checks to see that each main idea is numbered with a Roman numeral; each Roman numeral is followed by a period; the first word in each main idea begins with a capital letter.

I. ————————————
II. ————————————
III. ————————————

181. Two-Step Outline(I)   (1 or more players)

Materials: Same as for One-Step Outline, Game No. 180.

Directions: A player reads the story to complete a two-step outline. He checks to see that each main topic has a Roman numeral; each subtopic has a capital letter; each numeral and letter is followed by a period; the first word in each topic and subtopic begins with a capital letter.

I. ————————————
   A. ————————————
   B. ————————————
II. ————————————
   A. ————————————
   B. ————————————
   C. ————————————

V. CRITICAL AND CREATIVE THINKING

A. DRAWING CONCLUSIONS AND
   PREDICTING OUTCOMES

182. Before and After (P) (I)   (1 or more players)

Materials: Selected photographs, magazine pictures, comic strips.

Directions: A player examines a photograph, etc., and then gives his or her reaction to: What do you think happened before this photo was taken? What do you think happened afterward?

183. Anticipating the Outcome (P) (I)   (1 or more players)

Materials: Short stories without endings.

Directions: Ask players to make predictions about what will happen (or how the story will end). Then evaluate answers before reading the ending of the story.

184. Can You End It? (P)   (1 or more players)

Materials: Cards with short-short stories without endings.

Directions: A player reads the three or four line story and then creates an imaginative ending.

Example: Terry was a lazy cat. He slept while other cats had fun. One day Terry was asleep under an apple tree. When he awoke, he was surprised to see near him a ____ .

185. Pass (P) (I)   (3 or more players)

Materials: none.

Directions: The leader calls on a player to start telling a story. The leader then says, "Pass," and designates another player to continue the same story. When the story is completed, the players try to recall the entire story.

186. Finish the Story (P) (I)   (1 or more players)

Materials: Paper and pencil for each player.

Directions: The leader or teacher writes a few related sentences on the chalkboard, and then adds one or two questions to help develop the plot. Each player answers the questions to complete the story.

B. GIVING ILLUSTRATIONS OF YOUR OWN

187. Your Choice (P) (I)   (1 or more players)

Materials: none.

Directions: A player chooses any real or fictional character (from life, TV, a book, etc.) that is his or her favorite, and tells why this character or person is a favorite.

188. Write-a-Story Cards (P)   (1 or more players)

Materials: Make cards containing a picture and add several words.

Directions: A player uses a card in writing a story about the picture, incorporating the words on the card.

189. A Story About Me (P) (I)   (individual)

Materials: Ditto sheet or card with the following incomplete sentences.

Directions: The player completes each sentence in her or his own words.

1. My name is ———.
2. I am a ——————.
3. I go to ———.
4. I am ——— years old.
5. I am in the ——— grade.
6. My teacher's name is ——————.
7. I have ——— brothers.
8. I have ——— sisters.

Variation: For more able players, you might use questions such as these:

1. What is your name?
2. How old are you?
3. What is your home address?
4. In what state do you live?
5. Where do you go to school?
6. In what grade are you?
7. How many brothers and sisters do you have?

C. RELATING FACTS TO PAST EXPERIENCES

190. Thumbs Up — Thumbs Down (P) (group)

Materials: A set of flash cards, each with a single word — for the leader.

Directions: As the leader flashes a card, players put up their thumbs if they've done what the card "says;" thumbs down, if they haven't.

Examples: jumped, laughed, cat, store, sang, milk, flew.

Variations: Use cards labelled: "Good to Eat," and "Alive or Not."

191. Let's Go Back (P) (I) (individual)

Materials: Short-story cards.

Directions: The player reads the story and then tells a relating or similar story that had occured in the past to him or her.

Mary was excited. For the first time, she was given money to spend on anything she wanted. She bought roller skates for herself, and a ball game for her younger brother.

192. Just Like Me (P) (group)

Materials: none.

Directions: The first player makes a statement. The other players say, "Just like me," if they have had a similar experience. If not, the players say, "Not me." Players take turns making a statement. Two points are scored each time a player answers "Just like me." Examples:

I rode a train. I have a dog. I was noisy in class.

D. MAKING COMPARISONS

193. Comparing Characters in a Story (P) (I)   (1 or more players)

Materials: none.

Directions: After a player reads a story, she or he selects two characters from the story and tells how they were alike, and how they were different. A player writes a list of descriptive words for each character discussed.

194. Just Imagine (I)   (individual)

Materials: Cards with suppositions.

Directions: The player reads the cards and writes his or her own answers.

- Imagine you are a butterfly bursting through your cocoon.
- How does your body feel (as a butterfly)?
- What are you thinking? (as a butterfly)?
- What will you do after you have shed your cocoon? Why?

195. Real or Make Believe (P)   (1 or more players)

Materials: List of statements.

Directions: A player writes **real** or **make believe** after each statement. Examples:

>   The cat jumped over the moon.
>   Cats chase mice.
>   The frog changed into a prince.

196. How Are They Alike? (P) (I)   (1 or more players)

Materials: Cards with brief suggestions.

Directions: A player reads a comparison and then finishes the story in his or her own words.

People walked hurriedly along the busy city street.
Compare city life to an ant colony.

E. RECOGNIZING CAUSE AND EFFECT

197. Why? (P) (I)   (1 or more players)

Materials: Story or picture cards with questions.

Directions: A player examines the picture or reads the story and then tells what caused the character to behave as he or she did; what effect the character's action may have or had.

Examples: (1) John sat in the middle of 10 apple cores. He had a stomach ache. Why do you think John had the stomach ache?

   (2) Jenny was on her way to the candy store. On the way, she played tag with some friends. When she got to the store, she discovered that she had lost her money. What will Jenny have to do? Why? How do you think she feels?

198. What Must Have Happened? (P) (I)   (1 or more players)

Materials: Story cards.

Directions: A player reads a story and then decides what the cause was. Example:

   (1) John stood beside the puddle and looked at his muddy shoes.
   (2) Pat sat by the empty cookie jar, holding her sore stomach.

F. MAKING INFERENCES

199. Riddle Cards (P)   (1 or more players)

Materials: Four riddle cards with a number in the upper left corner; a large sheet of paper.

Directions: A player folds the paper in four parts or squares. The player selects a riddle card, reads the riddle, and writes (or draws) the answer to the riddle in the corresponding numbered square. Example:

I am in your house. I am in school, too. You can use me to talk to someone far away. You have heard me ring. (telephone)

200. Riddle Box (P)   (1 or more players)

Materials: Write a riddle on individual cards, and keep them in a box for players' use at any convenient time.

Directions: A player reads a riddle and then draws a picture to show the answer. Then the player can make up another riddle and add it to the riddle box. Examples:

I can sing.	I like to run.
I can fly.	I have a little house.
I have a nest.	I say, ''Bow-wow.''
(bird)	(dog)

201. Riddles and More Riddles (I)   (1 or more players)

Materials: Same as for Riddle Box, Game No. 200.

Directions: Players try to guess and write the answers.

> I know a word.
> It begins like **cut** and **cake**.
> It hangs on a window.
> What is it? (curtain)

What has four legs, one head, and a foot? (bed).
What runs but can't walk? (water—river—stream).

202. Summarizing (I)   (1 or more players)

Materials: Story cards of fact.

Directions: A player reads the story and crosses out any untrue sentence.

All pennies are made of copper. Copper wiring is good for electricity in your home. Some people have copper teakettles, and some people wear copper jewelry. Copper is made of pennies.

G. FORMING JUDGEMENTS AND OPINIONS

203. Fact or Opinion? (P) (I)   (1 or more players)

Materials: Story cards; sheet of paper and pencil for each player.

Directions: A player copies a story from the card and underlines only the factual sentences. Discuss why the other sentences are not facts.

Many plants grow from seeds. Some plants grow from bulbs or cuttings. I think seed plants are the best. John says that plants from bulbs are better.

Variation: Clip various advertisements from a newspaper, and discuss the content in terms of facts.

204. Is It Fact or Fiction? (P) (I)   (group)

Materials: Questions and answers for the leader. Panel members answer questions when called upon.

Directions: Two players compete as in "Hollywood Squares" TV game. The leader asks a question for a panel member to answer. A player decides which panel member is to answer the question, and then agrees or disagrees with that panel member's answer.

H. DETERMINING VALUE OF INFORMATION

205. TV News (P) (I) (1 or more players)

Materials: Paper and pencil for each player; script for the TV newscaster.

Directions: The newscaster reads his or her news report. Players make notes about statements they feel are one-sided or incorrect. Discussion should follow.

A space station orbits Earth. We are learning many space secrets and more about life on Earth from the crew in the space station. Unfortunately, only men are in the crew. Having our own space station is the best thing that has happened to this country. We can afford to spend millions of dollars more on this great space project.

206. Sense or Nonsense? (P) (group)

Materials: Questions and flash cards for the leader.

Directions: The leader asks a question and flashes a word card. Players reply be saying "sense" or "nonsense."

1. Would men play with this? (doll)
2. Can cowboys do this? (ride)
3. Do they live in a hen house? (children)
4. Would you like to ride in this? (plane)
5. Do cats like to eat this? (fish)

207. Make Believe (P) (3 or more players)

Materials: Cards with a set of directions for each player.

Directions: A player pantomimes or acts out the directions and the other players guess who the "actor" is. Example: Make believe you are a policewoman; a roller skater; a lively frog; an airplane; the teacher.

208. Silly Sentences (P) (2 or more players)

Materials: On the chalkboard or on cards, write **yes** and **no** generalizations.

Directions: A player indicates which generalization is false or silly by drawing a face after it. If the generalization is silly, the player draws a laughing mouth on the face. If the generalization is true, no drawing is needed.

Variation: This game can be played orally by having the players actually make a silly face after each false generalization is given. Example: My dog told me a spooky story.

209. What Makes Sense? (P) (I) (1 or more players)

Materials: Make cards with short paragraphs for each player.

Directions: A player copies the paragraph on a sheet of paper, omitting those sentences which have no bearing on the story or message.

I am going to the supermarket with my mother. We will buy food for our family. I push the cart in the store. The butcher cuts the meat. I help choose some of the foods. It is a sunny day, and I want ice cream. My mother pays for the food.

VI. LITERATURE INTERPRETATION AND STYLISTIC ELEMENTS

A. RECOGNIZING BEAUTY OF PHRASES AND WORDS

210. Word Pictures (P) (I)   (1 or more players)

Materials: List of descriptive phrases.

Directions: Players are given a list of descriptive words and are asked to write them as a finished group of phrases.

Example: his (best) friend

1. a___, ___night
2. a___, ___boy
3. a___, ___day
4. the___, ___news
5. the___, ___shore
6. a___, ___dog
7. a___, ___girl
8. a___, ___man
9. his___, ___friend
10. a___, ___house

dark	rough	happy	only	cold
winter	young	old	bent	wooden
rocky	deep	rainy	blue	wet
little	small	sad	warm	winter

211. Associating Words (P) (I)

Materials: List of descriptive words.

Directions: Players are given a list of descriptive words and write words that go with them. Example: warm   (day)

Adjectives:

sleepy	green	cold	white	best
big	dark	blue	high	warm
black	rainy	gray	little	wet
bumpy	pretty	happy	long	rough

Prepositions:

to	through	under	down	inside
on	above	after	before	around
by	behind	beside	across	at

Variation: Players make up silly phrases; scary phrases; unusual or beautiful phrases.

B. CREATING MENTAL IMAGES

212. Pantomime Words (P) (I)   (2 or more players)

Materials: A number of words written on flashcards spread along the chalk rail (happy, tired, cold, weary).

Directions: Each player silently chooses a word, and in turn, acts it out. Other players try to guess which word it is. The player to guess the pantomime word first does the next pantomime.

213. Make a Choice (I)   (individual)

Materials: Cards with questions and possible answers.

Directions: The player circles the answer which is more interesting to her or him. Then the player explains the choice made.
1. Which is more interesting—a rock or kite?
2. Which is more powerful—a rocket or water?
3. Which is lighter—a happy heart or a feather in the wind?
4. Which would you rather be without—ears or nose?
5. Which is more satisfying—a beautiful sunset or your favorite dessert?

214. What Did You See in Your Mind? (P) (I)   (2 or more players or teams)

Materials: Descriptive paragraphs or stories, and a list of questions.

Directions: Players or teams are given a paragraph or story to read. Players list all the things they could "see" in their minds as they read the selection. The player or team with the most items wins. Questions for mental pictures:

What did the character look like?   What was the weather like?
Where was the character going?   What sounds were heard?
What did the character see?   How did the character feel?

C. INTERPRETING FIGURATIVE LANGUAGE

215. If (P) (I)   (1 or more players)

Materials: Cards with initial suppositions.

Directions: A player finishes each supposition—in verse or prose.

> If I were a clown,   If I were a tree,
> I'd_____   I'd_____

216. Similes (P) (I)   (1 or more players)

Materials: List of unfinished sentences.

Directions: Players try to find as many different ways as they can to end each sentence sensibly. The player with the most endings wins.

1. The house is as warm as . . .
2. He is as big as . . .
3. She was as gentle as . . .
4. Mark is as slow as . . .
5. I am as hungry as . . .

Variation: Players may choose one sentence and illustrate it, or may choose to complete as many possible in a given length of time. Players add similes of their own.

217. Similes for Sentences (I)   (1 or more players)

Materials: List of similes.

Directions: Players are given a list of similes with the last word omitted. They supply the missing word and use the entire simile in a sentence. Examples:

as round as a (ball)   as wet as a (fish)
as straight as an (arrow)   as poor as a (rat)
as soft as (snow)   as strong as a (horse)
as pretty as a (picture)   as white as (snow, lily)
as black as (coal, night)   as tight as a (drum)
as free as a (bird)   as sick as a (dog)
as fierce as a (lion)   as blind as a (bat)
as cool as a (cucumber)   as warm as (toast)
as sharp as a (tack)   as clean as a (whistle)
as red as a (rose)   as sly as a (fox)

Variation: Players are given a picture clue to help them finish the similes.

218. Metaphors (I)   (1 or more players)

Materials: List of metaphors.

Directions: Players make as many metaphors as they can within a given time, and then tell what each metaphor means. Examples:

You are not the only pebble on the beach.
His whiskers are black thread.
Jake is a cool cat and Mary is a card.

Variation: Players write metaphors and illustrate them.

219. Create Metaphors (I) (2 or more players)

Materials: A sample of a metaphor to use as a guide.

Directions: Players use the sample to create metaphors of their own. Discussion should follow for each metaphor created.

1. The moon is a yellow ballon in the night sky.
2. A white, soft blanket covered the cold ground.
3. People rushed out of the building as ants run to a picnic.

D. IDENTIFY CHARACTERS AND RECREATE SCENES

220. Hunting for Action (P) (I)   (2 or more players)

Materials: Storybooks.

Directions: One player acts out a part of a story just read. The other players look for the place in the book that tells about the action. The player who finds the passage first may read it aloud.

Variation: After a short reading, players list all the action words in the story.

221. Mystery Guest (I)   (2 or more players)

Materials: none.

Directions: A player who is "it" dresses as a character in a well-known story. Other players ask questions which the character can answer with a yes or no (as in the TV game, "What's My Line?")

Variation: After players have guessed the name of the character, they can make a character analysis by checking some of the following:

patience	humility	philanthropy	mildness	creative
dishonest	stubborn	compassion	cowardly	curiosity
humor	greed	humanism	selfless	cowardly

E. APPRECIATE AUTHORS' LANGUAGE

222. How Do They Speak? (I)   (1 or more players)

Materials: Various stories; list of questions.

Directions: A player reads passages (or remembers) how certain authors have their characters speak. Example:

1. Which character speaks in exaggerations?
2. Which character finds something funny in everything?
3. Which author uses many adjectives to give description?
4. Which author uses similes and metaphors?

Variations: (1) Players use selected paragraphs or sentences from different expressions of English, and try to determine who is speaking; where and when the story took place.

a. "At that time, he said, a miracle would show who should be rightly king of all the realm."
a. "He charged them, also, by no means to be cruel but to give mercy unto him that asketh mercy."
b. "Say—I'm going in a-swimming, I am. Don't you wish you could? But of course you'd druther work—wouldn't you? Course you would!"
b. "Like it? Well, I don't see why I oughtn't to like it. Does a boy get a chance to whitewash a fence every day?"
   "Say, Tom, let me whitewash a little."
c. "How the British Regulars fired and fled,
   How the farmers gave them ball for ball,
   From behind each fence and farmyard wall,
   Chasing the red-coats down the lane,
   Then crossing the fields to emerge again
   Under the trees at the turn of the road,
   And only pausing to fire and load."
d. "By golly," said Jim, "this kind of weather is enough to stunt that little feller. Think I'll run him into camp and shove him under the shed where it is dry. Daggone if he don't look like he's just a few hours old, maybe born on the same minute that little Billy Roper was."

a. *Arthur Wins the Sword and Slays the Giant,* by Mary MacLeod
b. *The Adventures of Tom Sawyer,* by Mark Twain
c. *Paul Revere's Ride,* by Henry Wadsworth Longfellow
d. *Young Cowboy,* by Will James

Variation: (2) Players decide what kind of writer they are reading by applying the following questions to a book:

a. Does the author use long, compound or complex sentences — or short, declarative sentences?
b. Does the author put the main idea of a paragraph usually at the beginning, middle, or end of each paragraph?
c. Does the author use a lot of conversation or description?
d. Does the author write in the first or third person?

F. USE OF DIALOGUE

223. Real or Unreal Talk? (P) (I)   (1 or more players)

Materials: List of formal and informal sentences.

Directions: Players read the sentences and rewrite them in informal or real dialogue. Examples:

They invited me to go. However, I will not.
They asked me to go, but I won't.
He is the boy whom I saw in school.
I saw that boy in school.
They have eaten the entire thing.
They ate the whole thing. They ate it all.

Variation: Players are given a list of informal sentences and tell or write them formally.

224. Say It Short (P) (I)   (1 or more players)

Materials: Lists of formal and short or informal dialogue.

Directions: Players use the short dialogue and write what the whole sentence would be. Examples:

"Ouch   - I am exclaiming,   "Ouch!"
"What?"   "Good-by."
"Help!"   "Say!"
"Hi!"   "Henry!"
"Hello."   "Oh!"

Variation: Players change formal dialogue to informal.

G. EXAGGERATIONS AND QUAINT EXPRESSIONS

225. Is It True? (P)   (1 or more players)

Materials: List of questions.

Directions: Players answer the list of questions with a yes or no answer.

1. Can a boy jump over the sun?
2. Is grass green?
3. Can a house walk up stairs?
4. Can an orange taste?
5. Do you eat nails for dinner?
6. Can a rug get dirty?
7. Can an apple sing a song?
8. Can a desk study?
9. Can a girl do homework? thimble?
10. Can a giant sleep in a thimble?

226. Tall Tale (P) (I)   (group)

Materials: Tall tales for the leader (Paul Bunyon or class-created tall tales).

Directions: Players shout "Tall Tale" after each statement that is exaggerated—as told by the leader. Discussion should follow about why a sentence or paragraph is considered a tall tale.

227. Common Language (P) (I)   (1 or more players)

Materials: List of common expressions.

Directions: Players put common expressions into sentences and tell what each means. Example: I will tell you **straight from the shoulder**. (tell facts as they really are.)

1. all work and no play
2. better late than never
3. cold as ice
4. on the beam
5. easier said than done
6. green with envy
7. last but not least
8. white as a sheet
9. on the ball
10. bitter end

VII. DICTIONARY — GLOSSARY

A. ALPHABETICAL ORDER

228. Sequence (P) (1 or more players)

Materials: List of letters on the chalkboard; paper and pencil for each player.

Directions: The player copies the exercise from the board, and fills in each blank the missing letters of the alphabet.

a__c__e__g__i__k__m
o__q__s__u__w__y

229. Set Them Right (P) (I) (2 or more players or teams)

Materials: Make 2 sets of 10 word cards, each with a different word.

Directions: A player or team arranges a set of cards in alphabetical order as fast as they can. The first player or team to alphabetize a set of cards wins 10 points. Deduct 2 points for each card placed incorrectly.

Variation: As a player gains proficiency with alphabetizing the first letter of words, progress to second, third, and fourth letters of words.

230. Which Comes Before and After? (P)   (1 or more players)

Materials: Card with letters and blank spaces.

Directions: A player copies the information on the card and decides the missing letters that precede and follow the given letters.

__d__   __f__   __h__   __m__
__l__   __y__   __r__   __n__

231. A Word for Each Letter (P)   (1 or more players)

Materials: Players copy the letters of the alphabet or are given a Ditto sheet of it.

Directions: The players find a word in their reading books for each letter, and write the word beside the letter.

232. Picture Dictionary (P)   (1 or more players)

Materials: Shoe box and 5x7'' cards.

Directions: As a player learns a new word, he or she prints it on a card, draws a picture of it, and files the card alphabetically in the shoe box.

233. Let's Call Parents (P)   (1 or more players)

Materials: none.

Directions: Make believe you wish to call parents of players to invite them to school. Players are asked if Mrs. Smith's phone number would precede or follow Mrs. Wood's in the telephone directory.

234. Locating Words in Alphabetical Order (P) (I)

(2 teams or 2 players)

Materials: List of words to be rewritten in alphabetical order.

Directions: A team rewrites the words in alphabetical order and exchanges papers with another team who checks the alphabetical order with a dictionary (if necessary).

Variation: For less able players, provide a shorter list of words and have players circle each word that is out of order.

235. Class Directory (P)

(group)

Materials: Pencil and paper for each player.

Directions: A player lists all the girls' names in alphabetical order; all the boys' names in alphabetical order. A final, single list can be posted on the bulletin board.

236. Open the Dictionary (P) (I)

(group)

Materials: Dictionary for each player.

Directions: A player opens his or her dictionary at random, and states, "I have opened the dictionary to an "s" page." Each player gives a word whose initial sound is "s."

B. GUIDE WORDS

237. Parts of a Dictionary (P) (I)   (group)

Materials: Dictionary and list of words.

Directions: After players have been introduced to the four-part division (a—d, e—l, m—r, and s—z) they write the number (1, 2, 3, or 4) to show which part of the dictionary the word can be found.

wish __4__	parade____	rabbit _____
bean____	hotel _____	flea _____
nice _____	cash _____	trick_____

238. Exploring for Guide Words (I)   (2 or more players)

Materials: Dictionary; paper and pencil for each player.

Directions: Each player writes a list of words. He then exchanges papers with another player who must fill in the blanks.

Between what two Guide Words would you find these words in the dictionary?

_____ straight _____   _____ holiday_____

C. SYLLABICATION

239. How Many Syllables? (P) (I)   (1 or more players)

Materials: Ditto sheet with words and headings.

Directions: A player writes the correct number under each heading.

WORDS	VOWELS SEEN?	VOWELS HEARD?	NO. OF SYLLABLES?
basket	_____	_____	_____
funny	_____	_____	_____
family	_____	_____	_____
people	_____	_____	_____

240. Key to Pronunciation (i)   (1 or more players)

Materials: Dictionary and list of words for each player.

Directions: Players used the abbreviated key at the bottom of a word page. They find the word in the dictionary and check how the vowel should be pronounced.

Words to Find   **Underline One**

  mariner   sat   fare

241. Pronunciations (I)   (1 or more players)

Materials: Dictionary and list of words for each player.

Directions: Players find the words in the dictionary, and write the pronunciation as it appears in the parenthesis.

D. ACCENT MARKS

242. Mark the Stress (I)   (1 or more players)

Materials: Dictionary and list of words for each player.

Directions: Use the dictionary and mark the primary and secondary stress marks after the correct syllables.

     jun ior   twen ty   trea ty

E. MULTIPLE MEANINGS

243. Dictionary Words (P)   (individual)

Materials: Fold a half sheet of easel paper into six squares. On 3x5'' cards, list and number six nouns found in a picture dictionary.

Directions: In each square, a player writes a number, a sentence containing the word, and makes as illustration.

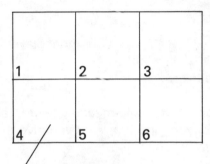

1. apple	2. bee
3. cat	4. hat
5. king	6. whale

Mother had a new hat.

244. Vocabulary Build-Up (P) (I)   (1 or more players)

Materials: Paper and pencil for each player.

Directions: A player writes (illustrates) a word in as many ways as he can. Example: dwelling—cabin, hut, barn, tent, cave, doghouse, motel, skyscraper, farmhouse.

245. Dictionary Game (P) (I)   (1 or more players or teams)

Materials: Dictionary for each team; chalk for the leader.

Directions: The leader writes a word on the chalkboard. A member of each team holds the dictionary. The first one to find the word and use it in a sentence, suggests another word for the groups to find and use.

246. Which Meaning? (I)   (1 or more players)

Materials: Dictionary for each player.

Directions: The leader mentions a multiple-meaning word (as light) and uses it in a sentence. Players find the word and give the correct meaning of it, as fast as they can.

247. Prove It (I)   (1 or more players)

Materials: Dictionary and list of questions and answers.

Directions: A player answers each question, using the dictionary to prove his answers.

This $20.00 bill is a counterfeit.
Does counterfeit mean fake or minted?

248. Write Questions (I) (2 or more players)

Materials: Dictionary for each player; pencil and paper.

Directions: Each player writes questions that could be answered by a YES or NO answer. The player then gives the question to another player who checks the dictionary to answer the questions.

Is the capital of Nebraska in Lincoln?
Are the Bahamas in the Atlantic Ocean?

249. Abstract Words (I) (1 or more players)

Materials: List of paired sentences; dictionary.

Directions: A player reads each sentence and tells what the underlined word means. A dictionary is consulted to prove the answers.

1. Did you **record** the figures in the book?
   I played the same **record** three times.
2. Did he **rebel** at your command?
   He was the **rebel** of our family.
3. I **object** to what she had said.
   He put an **object** into his pocket.

250. Like or Unlike? (I) (1 or more players)

Materials: Dictionary and list of words to look up.

Directions: Players race in finding meanings of words, and write **like** or **unlike** after each pair of words:

enthusiasm — impression   strike — run
systematic — orderly   artificial — unreal

VIII Word Lists

Picture Words — Initial Consonant Sounds

B

baby
bag
baker
ball
balloon
banana
barrel
barn
basket
bat
beans
bear
beaver
bed
beets
bell
belt
bench
berries
bib
bicycle
bird
boat
bone
book
boots
bottle
bow
bowl
box
boy
bubbles
buffalo
bus
butterfly
buttons

Soft C

celery
bent
centipede
circle

Hard C

cabin
cactus
cage
cake
calendar
camel
camera
can
candle
candy
cane
cannon
canoe
cap
cape
car
carriage
carrots
castle
cat
coat
coconut
collar
comb
cone
corn
cow
cucumber
cup

D

daffodil
daisy
deer
desk
dice
dinosaur
dish
dog
doll
door
doughnut
duck

F

fan
feather
feet
fence
fifteen
fifty
fingers
fire
fireman
fireplace
fish
five
foot
football
fork
forty
fountain
four
fourteen
fox
funnel

Soft G

giraffe
gerbil

Hard G

garage
gate
geese
girl
goat
goldfish
golfclub
goose
gorilla
guitar
gun

H

hammer
hammock
hanger
harp
hat
hay
heart
helmet
helicopter
hen
hippo
hive
hook
horn
horse
horseshoe
hose
hydrant

J

jacket
jacks
jar
jet
jug
jumprope

K

kangaroo
kettle
key
king
kite
kitten

L

ladder
lamb
lamp
leaf
leg
lemons
leopard
letter
lion
lips
lobster
lock
log

M

magnet
mailman
man
mask
matches
mittens
money
monkey
moon
moose
mop
moth
mouse

N

nails
necklace
needle
nest
net
newspaper
nine
nineteen
nose
nurse
nuts

P

paddle
pail
pan
panda
parachute
peach
peacock

pear
peas
pen
pencil
penguin
piano
pie
pig
pin
pineapple
pipe
pirate
pitcher
policeman
pony
popcorn
porcupine
pot
potatoes
pumpkin
puppet
purse

R

rabbit
raccoon
radio
rake
rat
rattle
record
refrigerator
ring
robot
rocket
roof
rooster
rope

rubbers
rug
ruler

S

saddle
safe
sandwich
scissors
seal
seven
seventeen
sink
six
sixteen
socks
submarine
suit
suitcase
sun

T

table
tail
teeth
telephone
television
ten
tent
tie
tiger
tire
toes
tomato
top
tulip

V

vase
vest
vine
violin

W

wagon
watermelon
web
window
witch
woman
worm

Y

yarn
yo-yo

Z

zebra
zipper

Consonant Blends—Picture Words

bl

blanket
blimp
blocks
blouse

br

bread
bride
bridge
broom
brush

cl

clam
claw
clip
clock
cloud
clown

cr

crab
cradle
crayons
crib
crocodile
cross
crow
crown

dr

dragon
dress
drum

fl

flag
flashlight
flower
flowerpot
flute
fly

fr

frame
frog
fruit

gl

glass
glasses
globe
gloves

gr

grapes
grasshopper

pl

plane
plate
pliers
plow
plum

pr

present
pretzel
prince
princess

sk

skates
skeleton
skirt
skis

sl

sled
slide
slipper

sn

snail
snake
snowman
snowshoes
snowsuit

sp

spaceship
spacesuit
spear
spider
spool
spoon

st

stairs
stamp
staple
star
statue
stocking
store
stove

sw

swan
sweate
swing

tr

tracks
train
tree
truck
trumpet
trunk

Picture Words for Initial Digraphs

ch	sh	th	wh
chain	sheep	thimble	whale
chair	shelf	thirteen	wheel
cheese	shell	thirty	wheelbarrow
cherries	ship	thistle	whip
chicken	shirt	thumb	whistle
chimney	shoes		
chipmunk	shovel		
church			

Short Vowel Sounds — Picture Words

a	e	i	o	u
ant	bed	bricks	blocks	brush
apple	bell	bridge	box	bus
bat	belt	clip	clock	crutch
calf	chest	crib	dog	cup
can	desk	dish	doll	drum
cat	dress	fish	fox	duck
clam	eggs	king	frog	gun
fan	fence	lips	lock	jug
flag	jet	mill	log	nuts
glass	men	pig	mop	plum
hand	nest	pin	ox	rug
hat	net	ring	pot	sun
lamp	pen	ship	socks	truck
man	shells	whip	top	tub
match	sled	witch		
pan				
stamp				
tacks				

Long Vowel Sounds — Picture Words

a	e	i	o	u
cage	beans	bike	boat	cube
cake	bee	bride	bone	flute
cane	beet	dice	coat	fruit
cape	cheese	file	comb	mule
chain	feet	five	cone	suit
gate	key	kite	globe	tube
grapes	leaf	mice	goat	
nail	peach	nine	nose	
pail	queen	pie	rope	
plane	seal	tie	rose	
plate	sheep		smoke	
rake	tree			
safe	wheel			
skate				
snake				
snail				
table				
train				
vase				
whale				

Long Vowel Combinations

ai

aid
braid
laid
paid
raid

bail
fail
frail
hail
jail
mail
nail
pail
quail
rail
snail
tail
trail

aim
claim

brain
chain
drain
gain
grain
main
pain
plain
rain
stain
train

paint
faint

air
chair
fair
flair
hair
lair
pair
stair

ea

beach
peach
reach
teach

pea
sea
tea

bead
lead
read

beak
bleak
creak
leak
peak
sneak
speak
teak
weak

deal
meal
real
seal
steal
veal

beam
cream
dream
steam
stream
team

bean
clean
Jean
mean

cheap
heap
leap

clear
dear
ear
fear
gear
hear
near
rear
smear
spear

beast

east
least

beat
cheat
eat
heat
meat
neat
seat
treat
wheat

Long Vowel Combinations

ee		oa
bee	peel	load
fee	reel	road
free	steel	toad
tee	wheel	
tree		cloak
wee	green	croak
	preen	soak
bleed	queen	
breed	seen	foam
creed	sheen	roam
deed		
feed	cheep	groan
greed	creep	loan
head	deep	moan
need	keep	
seed	peep	boast
speed	seep	coast
steed	sheep	roast
tweed	sleep	toast
weed	steep	
	weep	
beef	beet	
reef	feet	
	fleet	
cheek	greet	
creek	meet	
meek	sheet	
peek	sleet	
seek	sweet	
sleek		
week	breeze	
	cheese	
creel	freeze	
eel	sneeze	
feel		
heel		

Common Rhyming Words

ab	**ag**	**am**	**and**
cab	bag	clam	band
dab	brag	dam	bland
gab	drag	ham	brand
jab	flag	jam	gland
nab	gag	ram	grand
slab	hag	tam	hand
stab	lag	yam	land
	rag		sand
	sag		stand

ack	tag	**ame**	
back	lag	blame	
black		came	**ang**
crack	**age**	dame	bang
jack		fame	clang
pack	cage	flame	fang
sack	page	frame	gang
shack	rage	lame	hang
slack	sage	name	pang
smack	stage	tame	rang
	wage		sang

ad	**ake**	**an**	
add	bake	ban	**ank**
bad	cake	can	bank
cad	fake	clan	blank
dad	flake	fan	frank
fad	lake	man	hank
glad	make	pan	rank
had	rake	plan	sank
lad	sake	ran	spank
mad	stake	span	tank
pad	take	tan	thank
sad	wake	van	yank

ap	aw	each	ent
cap	caw	beach	bent
flap	claw	bleach	cent
gap	draw	breach	dent
lap	jaw	peach	lent
map	law	preach	meant
nap	paw	reach	rent
rap	raw	teach	sent
sap	saw		tent
snap			went
tap		eat	
trap	all	beat	
	ball	feat	eek
	call	heat	beak
	fall	meat	cheek
ark	gall	neat	leak
bark	hall	peat	leek
dark	mall	pleat	meek
hark	tall	seat	peek
lark	wall		seek
mark		ed	week
park		bed	
shark	ay	bread	
	bay	dead	est
	day	dread	best
ash	gay	fed	guest
cash	gray	fled	jest
clash	hay	head	nest
crash	Jay	lead	pest
dash	lay	Ned	rest
hash	may	red	test
mash	pay	sled	west
rash	play	Ted	zest
sash	pray	thread	
	say	wed	
	way		

ell
bell
cell
Nell
nell
sell
shell
tell
well
yell

et
bet
get
jet
let
met
net
pet
set
wet

en
Ben
den
hen
Ken
men
pen
ten
yen

ice
dice
lice
mice
nice
rice
slice
spice
twice

end
bend
blend
friend
lend
mend
send
tend
trend
vend

ill
bill
dill
frill
gill
grill
hilll
kill
mill
pill

in
bin
chin
fin
grin
kin
pin
shin
sin
skin
tin
win

ine
brine
dine
fine
line
mine
nine
pine
shine
vine
wine

ing
bring
cling
ding
fling
king
ping
ring
sing
sting
swing

thing
wing

ip
clip
dip
drip
flip
hip
lip
nip
rip
sip
ship
skip
slip
tip
trip
whip
zip

it
bit
fit
hit
knit
lit
pit
quit
sit
slit
wit

ock	ot	ug	un
block	cot	bug	bun
clock	dot	dug	fun
dock	got	drug	gun
flock	hot	hug	pun
knock	jot	jug	run
lock	lot	lug	sun
mock	not	mug	spun
rock	plot	plug	stun
sock	rot	rug	
shock	shot		
stock	tot		

um

bum
gum
glum
hum
mum
plum
rum
sum
slum

old	ow
bold	bow
cold	blow
fold	flow
gold	glow
hold	low
mold	mow
sold	row
told	sow
	show
	snow
	stow

ook

book
brook
cook
crook
hook
look
nook
rook
shook
took

oy

boy
coy
joy
ploy
Roy
soy
toy

ump

bump
clump
dump
hump
jump
lump
pump
plump
stump

Index